# Thriving In Turbulent Times

*With Contributions From 8 World Famous Leaders including 2 Superstars from the Movie 'The Secret'*

I0161421

Hosted by
## Raymond Aaron

World Prosper Summit
April 24 & 25, 2020
Day 1 of 2

**10-10-10**
Publishing

Thriving In Turbulent Times – Series 1 (Raw unedited - Day 1 of 2)

www.WorldProsperSummit.com/livestream

Copyright © 2020

ISBN: 978-1-77277-355-2

**Limits of Liability and Disclaimer of Warranty**

The author and publisher shall not be liable for your misuse of the enclosed material. This book is strictly for informational and educational purposes only. Content and wording has been transcribed from a live event and is raw unedited version, product was presented at the time of the event.

**Warning – Disclaimer**

The purpose of this book is to educate and entertain. The author and/or publisher do not guarantee that anyone following these techniques, suggestions, tips, ideas, or strategies will become successful. The author and/or publisher shall have neither liability nor responsibility to anyone with respect to any loss or damage caused, or alleged to be caused, directly or indirectly by the information contained in this book.

Publisher
10-10-10 Publishing
Markham, ON
Canada

Printed in Canada and the United States of America

# Table of Contents

# Being Up in Down Times

## Mark Victor Hansen

**Raymond Aaron:**

. . . famous co-creator with Jack Canfield of the entire Chicken Soup for the Soul series of books. If you think that's a big handle, wait til you hear this handle. Mark Victor Hansen is the number one, nonfiction author of all time. His talk is the most uplifting talk you could ever imagine. That's why he asked to go first. His talk is staying up during downtime. Mark Victor Hansen, you have 30 minutes to set the stage and bring everybody out. Go for it.

**Mark Victor Hansen:**

Good. Hi everybody. It's Mark Victor Hansen here. I'm elated to be Raymond Aaron's friend forever and now your friend. I really do want to talk to you about How to be Up in Down Times. We're going to do three basic things. First, I'm going to show you where $50 trillion worth of business is going to come to pass during the next decade. We are going to get a lot. Raymond said, "We're going to repivot. We're going to reinvent. We're going to reposition ourselves, and it really starts in the mind."

**Mark Victor Hansen:**

Because some of you who've been with me in seminars around the world know that the cliche is what you think about comes about. What we're going to do is think about positive things that are going to change the world. Then we can talk a little bit about why you can have success if you know where your destiny is and you learn that by asking. Then last but not least, I'm going to encourage every one of you, during this downtime, to write your book, because every one of you has a book in you. I just think there's more in you than you've ever thought before.

**Mark Victor Hansen:**

Let's start at a big high level. Charles Darwin, who famously taught the principle called survival of the fittest said, "It's not the strongest of the species. It's not the most intelligent that survive. It's the one most adaptable to change." All of us, eight billion of us, not just those of us watching here, but eight billion of us have had simultaneously thrust change on us, because we've all been incarcerated. I'm going to do a great story about that and show you how to get out of it, and I'm going to show you how we're going to break out of this in a few minutes. We all know that hurricane winds and trees either bend and survive or break from their rigidity during any challenge.

**Mark Victor Hansen:**

Every one of us right now has got to be bendable, habitable, and transformable. All the companies I own, and I own four big companies, got to be unique. They got to be original. They got to be transformational. I want you to get out of the pressures and make sure you're not going to break during this. When we're being adaptable, I'm saying you've got to be able to think. You got to be able to move> you got to be a little faster.

You got to have more wisdom than anytime in history. While you're at World Prosper Summit, is to gain that wisdom, right? Because you got 19 eclectically wise. I think every one of them is a friend of mine.

**Mark Victor Hansen:**

They're ready to help you adapt and go beyond survival to extraordinary thriving. Because there's ability here. Yeah, we got a pandemic, but we've had recessions before. Every one of us had some personal crisis or other. All of us have had to start over one time or another, if you're over 20 years old probably. That's happened throughout the ages. Everyone's been fraught with challenges and opportunity. As long as that's going to happen . . . And we're going to have more. We're going to have floods. We're going to have earthquakes. We're going to have war's, plights, plagues, market crash and the like. Our ancestors survive and ultimately thrive. Therefore, that means that you got that in your genes. You've got it in your genetic code. You've got it into your awareness that you can cut the mustard and do it.

**Mark Victor Hansen:**

Now I've written a little booklet with Mitzi Perdue. You know her Perdue Chicken. They only do 22 million chickens a week, if you get it at Costco or Whole Foods or whatever, but she's written 4,000 major articles. Graduate of Harvard, 1963. She and our son Preston and I have written How to be Up in Down Times. I want to give it to you free and will tell you that at the end if you're interested. But the simple truth is that every one of us needs a new GPS to stay well, to stay safe, to stay on track, to come out stronger, better, smarter, and have foundational hope during this transformational journey. I want to incentivize you to stay alive, to go through the struggle, go through the adversity and arrive at the end, because every one of you has a destiny that's great.

**Mark Victor Hansen:**

If you're alive, your destiny isn't built. I'm going to help you unpack it so you can see where to do it. Then I want you to think of bigger, better, more innovative stuff than you've ever thought of before that's going to be breakthrough stuff. So immediately you'll feel better and you'll trust that you're going to have a glorious, worthwhile penultimate of futures. Because I've gone through the ups and downs of life. I'm 72 years old. I feel better than ever. I'm going to live to be 127 with options for renewal. What I want to do is give you the big picture, because when I was in graduate school at Bucky Fuller for seven years, he said, "You go from macro to micro, universe to this specific deductive to inductive."

**Mark Victor Hansen:**

I want you to understand there's grand opportunities, because there's grand challenges happening to us. Long ago, when I was working for Raymond, one time I'd just done the new tapes, that were the best seller at [inaudible 00:05:00], How to Think Bigger Than You Ever Thought You Could Think? They were being distributed again and we re-upped them and made them a little bit better enough to today. The challenge is, how big is your thinking? Because we are going into the most enormous problems ever. Now, let me just talk about it in terms of two major Seminole . . . Seminoles. Symbols. These are r lips, ladies and gentlemen. Symbols that every one of you are familiar with. Almost everyone knows in Raymond value, we're talking about a second ago, the ying and the yang. It's sort of a circle with a little S and in the single.

**Mark Victor Hansen:**

It's lasted for over 6,000 years, but it's verifiably true. This symbol literally means crisis equals opportunity. Therefore, if we have the biggest crisis, which we all are experiencing whether we want to or not, we also have the biggest opportunities. I'm going to talk about how to cash those by having you ask the right question, if you don't mind my saying so. I'm going to ask you to be awake, thoughtful, positive, and choose to transform, or you wouldn't be on this show with myself and 19 peers and Raymond. Right? All the companies I've done, in books like One Minute Millionaire, have always had the second symbol, which is a symbol of freedom, which is the butterfly, which I got a lot of butterfly symbols throughout my homes and offices, but it's a universal symbol of freedom.

**Mark Victor Hansen:**

My wife and I believe the triangle is, you've got to have your health, have your love, have your freedom. I hope you agree with that, but we want to have more freedom. We want to adapt wisely and position ourselves for increases of freedom. Remember, you can't look at a Caterpillar and predict butterfly, right? Likewise, you can't look at this crisis. It's simultaneous got eight billion of us within lockdown, and not see that a butterfly's going to emerge as we get released from total, worldwide, government-imposed cocoon. We're all in a cocoon. We're about to emerge as butterflies as far as I'm concerned.

**Mark Victor Hansen:**

Now, since 1776, the American Articles of Confederation, we've had 47 recessions. 1998, we had a major depression in America. In 20 to 29, we had The Great Depression. Now notice, in 1898, the depression had four innovations bust out and create what was called The Industrial Revolution. We have the automobile, Henry Ford. Edison created electricity and it telephoned the Wright brothers. Then after that crash came, we had the Wright brothers fly. Then the next one in 29 was monopoly, was created by Clarence Darrow, the guy that did The Scopes Trial. Then we had the computer. Then we had the jet.

**Mark Victor Hansen:**

Then we had the breakthrough of Gordon Moore's law which said, "Hey wait a second. Computer processor speeds double in effectiveness and halve in price every two years. That has consistently brought the price down." When I was back in university, computers were as big as my house, and now you know you've got more computing power Buzz Aldrin tells me in my cell phone than he did going to the moon in 1968 or 69. Look, we're in the most vast, virtually immediate, profitable, invisible, technological breakthroughs ever. I'm going to talk about two that are going to help us release from this incarceration.

**Mark Victor Hansen:**

The point is, you and I are going to make it through. Everyone that's watching is going to make it through. The crisis and setback don't get us unless we let it. We're going to let them be set forth for these extraordinary, looming opportunities. I'm going to ask you to proceed. Yes, I'm going to encourage you. Like Raymond said, to reset, to pivot, to have plan B, to reinvent yourself, to decide to contribute a new, exciting, wonderful, opportunistic, promotional ways for yourself and everyone else. Look, a decade ago there were a lot of companies we didn't know that are now Uber. Billion-dollar companies like

Uber and pretty soon Uber Air and Airbnb and Instagram and Square.

**Mark Victor Hansen:**

I predict we're going to have hundreds of those that are being conceived right now, some of them by you all. We're signing document. We didn't have a thing called DocuSign. Now, when I sell a piece of real estate or buy something, it comes to me, get signed. I never even meet the people in the transaction. In the old days, we had what was called a closing room. It was a waste of time. You had to go to the office and get it all done. Things are going like that, and they're going to keep changing. They'll change for you if you think they will. The law of attraction, which some of my peers are going to be teaching you, could have ended a secret.

**Mark Victor Hansen:**

Now, the point is, I want you to be a creative innovator that decides to contribute to transforming our world in a most magnificent of all possible ways and solve problems. Just decide what you're going to fix, what you want to make better, how you want to be happier than you've ever been. Because we're going to go through colossal change. You're going to say, "What am I going to do that I will get paid substantially for doing? What am I willing to fix that I see can be fixed?" You don't have to have an MBA, although I redefine that be a massive bank account rather, right, or a millionaire's bank account is even better. Raymond and I've talked about that in past and agree.

**Mark Victor Hansen:**

What is happening? It's going to vastly shape our world. First of all, we've become to a video centric world. Almost all the world now got a smartphone. We've got 5 billion people getting smartphones around the world, so everyone's going become podcasting centric. Right now, we have, just in the United States, 800,000 podcasters. Americans are listened to 157 million podcasts a day. Average American seven podcasts a week. It's sort of a mind blow. We got 3D avatar pop-up artwork coming to pass. I want to talk about seven businesses are going to do 50 trillion, not billion, trillion during this decade, and all you've got to say is, "How am I going to participate in it?"

**Mark Victor Hansen:**

Number one, we're going to turn trash into cash. That's my cliché of a company I'm part of. I'm an advisor to QCI in Michigan, and they're able to recapture 99% of all the atoms and molecules from garbage in landfills. We've got 10,000 closed landfills in America that are going to kill us if we don't, and it's going to be trillions of dollars of [inaudible 00:11:02] and assets. We're going to turn pollution into a resource, stop poisoning our water, and go to virtually unlimited fuel. We're going to turn fuel back to fuel of any type. We're going to turn water back to water, plastic back the plastic, 99% in metal back the metal. It's going to be monetized with all the gigantic levels. It's already started. It just happened to get temporarily stopped. A guy worked on it for 20 years, spent $300 million, and it's changing the world.

**Mark Victor Hansen:**

Number two, AI, artificial intelligence. It's called super computing. We see it in our smartphone. You see it in your GPS where you punch in, "I want to go to Raymond's house," and go [inaudible 00:11:40] and takes you. If you miss it, it doesn't say, "Slam on the brakes," just says, "Turn it the next time and go back and fix it up." It does it in a nanosecond.

We now know that IBM's Watson computer can out-think the human mind and make transactions that really think, but it takes a human mind that has to be ethical and take us to the next level.

**Mark Victor Hansen:**

Number three, we got the advent of coming. Everything has positive and negative, but 5G. That means super computing. It's going to be virtually instantaneous. You'll be able to download a three-hour movie into your smartphone while you're traveling at 40,000 feet, assuming like Raymond just said, we're going to be traveling on jets again. I think we are because of some of the things I'm going to tell you in a second. It's going to be the fastest, the best, and the biggest, and we're going to have new winners.

**Mark Victor Hansen:**

Next, number four, when I sold Chicken Soup for the Soul with Jack Canfield who will be on later, I bought a company called Natural Power Concepts. We made devices like pop up urban windmills that go 360 degrees, that use swarming technology. We got pulsating waves. We can have unlimited water, because you got to have energy to have water, water to have food, food to have abundance, abundance you have fundamental freedom. For the first time in this decade, I'm going to work on creating a 100% of humanity's economic and physical success with all these innovations. Now obviously, I'm a founder and investor and an owner and chairman of that.

**Mark Victor Hansen:**

Number five, we're going into a brand-new time with robots and cobots. A robot, you know what it does. It's going to do all the menial, the hard, the disgraceful, the dirty, the smelly, the ugly work that's been relegated to some people, and now those people are going to be freed and they're going to be running cobots, collaborative robots, that no one wanted to do, but one guy or lady will be fast trained, get certification at some of these schools that I'm part of, and we're going to be able to make whatever we want.

**Mark Victor Hansen:**

Like right, one of them companies I'm going to tell you about, we're making a mask that's made with nanoparticle tourmaline that rejects all virus, rejects all microbes, and those are going to be out starting in the next two weeks. It's amazing. We didn't need it before, but now we needed it and this is a way to do it. The truth is, everyone says, "Well, robots are going to take away business." No. I learned from Warren Buffet that, when he was born, 98% of people were in farm. 2% worked in intellectual property and white collar as you call it, or light blue collar. I like brighter colors. But anyhow, the point is now, look, we've had the biggest unemployment ever and it's not [inaudible 00:14:08].

**Mark Victor Hansen:**

Number six, IOT, Internet of Things. We're going to connect 50 billion devices: your home, your computer, your car, all of it's going to be connected. It won't be just Bill Gates who walks into his house and the music he wants comes in, when his wife walks in, music she wants. We're going into a new reality that's more exciting than ever before. Number seven, multi-dimensional transportation. We're going from constipated traffic jams, which one reason I moved out to California, because I couldn't stand. It took me three or four hours to get to LA from Newport beach. It just doesn't work.

**Mark Victor Hansen:**

At the consumer electronics show, I saw the first 3D cars. Then all of a sudden, I sat at dinner with the guy who invented them right here. The invention laboratory for bowling is here. It's a brilliant guy. Charlie [inaudible 00:00:14:55], 38 major inventions. He's got a jet that'll leave Arizona, where I live, and go all the way, in 20 minutes, to Mumbai or to Shanghai or to Australia. We're in an exciting time to breakthrough. Yeah, we got broken down supply chains, and we're going to have to outsource and bring them new, but we're going to bring them new with 3D printing, I predict, robots, cobots. All of you got to ask, "How am I going to participate in all that stuff?"

**Mark Victor Hansen:**

I want to stay in touch with you and tell you all these things are going to happen, because we're in the most gigantic resurgence ever. We're going to have new jobs, new opportunities. There's going to be plentiful stuff for those of us who are awake, of form, enthusiastic, and take self-determination to independent action. You've got to be enthused. That's why I asked Raymond if I could beat on my chest, get you to start thinking bigger, thinking new thinking extraordinary thoughts, because that's why you're here. You were born over a doubt of 18 billion brain cells waiting to go to work. We're going to overcome every obstacle.

**Mark Victor Hansen:**

We're going to over, under, around, or through and get to the other side. Why? Because the individuals on this show have brilliant, innovative, ingenuity. What I said is self determination to action, where I'm asking you to be a brave beacon on the hill. Yeah, I got 59 number one New York Times Bestsellers, more than anyone else alive on the planet according to Guinness Book of Records. I understand what it's like to work. I've written 309 bestselling books, and I'm going to keep writing. The point is, you and I can prevail. We can overcome anything, and we can overcome any nay-saying. You got to be careful. No more than 15 minutes of negative news. Peter Diamandis calls the CNN, The Crisis News Network. Well when I went bankrupt in 1974, I was reading the New York Times that says, "All the news fit to print."

**Mark Victor Hansen:**

It should have been all bad news fit to print, because it'll just spoil you. It'll destroy you. It'll make you depressed, despondent. It'll crush your spirit. That's why I'm so thankful that Raymond's doing the show, so we have people put their shoulders back, they breathe in, they start to go. Even our government's trying to save itself by all of our Congress and Senators all at home making a vote. They voted for two trillion, now $4.8 trillion to get people back to work, but they're not letting them work. That's what's amazing. Until we get this mask is one of two things is going to happen. I'm also part of a company called Virus Care, which I can't talk very much about it yet, but in the next two weeks amazing things are going to break through. That's why you got to remember that the last four letters of American, and I know Raymond's a Canadian, but American is, "I can. I can, will, and prevail."

**Mark Victor Hansen:**

What I'm saying is you can think up in down times. Matter of fact, you have to All those guys I talked about at first, the automobile, the electricity, airplanes, all came out of a depression. Why? I'm saying to you, I want you to think happy thoughts. I want you to go to new places. I want you to understand there's new possibilities for you that you've never even thought of. Other than this little book I wrote called Ask, which I'd encourage you to get, we want to give you free, How to be Up in Down Times, if you go to receiption@markvictorhansen.com, but also want you to consider writing a book, because books are the wealth of the nation .It depends on the quality of your writing and the quantity, but books are funded every level for me, and I hope for you.

**Mark Victor Hansen:**

I hope you like mine, and I hope you enjoy and start to write, because writings obviously been my right livelihood since I was 16 years old, but I want all of you to write a book for credibility. It gives you pride. It gives you a respect. It gives you a appreciation of adoring clients, friends, and you get to do stuff, because you'll have celebrity, you'll have authority. It'll be the most extraordinary door opener you've ever even considered. You'll improve your life, your lifestyle. Yeah, you can either write alone, or like I wrote with Jack, and then I wrote three books with Raymond, and we did Chicken Soup for the Canadian Soul.

**Mark Victor Hansen:**

Or you could have it ghost written, where you just come up with the concepts, and let somebody else, anything from an English professor to a real ghost writer help you out. Today, it's easy to find. When Jack and I were doing it, it was hard. The internet was just starting, the.com thing was just starting, and desktop publishing was just starting today. Book publishing is profitable. It's easy. You can upload reports, articles, chapters, like that thing I'm giving you, How to be Up in Down Times. We wrote it in the last six weeks actually, but we'll give it to you free. If you go to Amazon, you're going to have to pay $4.97 for it. I want you to have it free. But you say, "Well, do authors make money?" Well, J.K. Rowling's now the richest woman in Britain, so I guess she's done well.

## Mark Victor Hansen:

Obama just got paid $65 million to write his book. But let's even talk about something easier to do, like doing an interview. Any one of you could interview people and become successful. Napoleon Hill was one of my heroes. I read his book every time for the last 40 years. He interviewed the 500 most important people: businessmen, politicians, everything, introduced by none other than my hero, Andrew Carnegie. I hope you've been to his house of 95th and 5th Avenue and seen in the window. It says, "Authors are the wealth of the world. No man or woman gets rich without enriching all others." Great stuff. The first depression, 1898, America's written out by Wallace Wattles. He wrote the The Science of Getting Rich.

## Mark Victor Hansen:

Then Napoleon Hill wrote us out of the depression in 1937 while he was writing all the fireside chats for FDR, he wrote lines like, "You have nothing to fear, but fear itself," and "Quiet fears make it disappear." Well, a soothsayer told me, and I thought I should tell you this, that I was going to write the financial books to get us out of this. Obviously, I'm giving you a free book, How to be Up in Down Times, but I wrote One Minute Millionaire and I've written Richest Kids in America. Now we've just been contracted, as of two days ago, to write Richest Kids in America Two. I want every one of your kids to work. I want everybody to be an entrepreneur. I want everyone to know that they can create, develop, manifest their full potential and fulfill their destiny.

**Mark Victor Hansen:**

When you do die though, your obituary has your name, your age, and then the next thing it comes as books. This is before your business, before your family, before your life, before whatever you've accomplished, before whatever you invented. Do books make the world work? Heck yeah. Do books change the world? Yeah. Do books last forever and leave a lasting legacy? The answer's yes. Do they enable you to serve greatly with love at levels you hadn't thought? Yeah. Are they fun? Well, yeah. If you decide they're fun, they're fun. I happen to really be addicted to writing. I wake up in the middle of the night and I can't think enough. Books have had me literally travel around the world and meet all the world leaders. I've worked in China until three years ago, 22 years in a row, four times a year, paid 75 grand and sold 374 million books in China. I'm not happy with China today for a lot of reasons, but that's a whole different issue.

**Mark Victor Hansen:**

Look, books solve problems, improve circumstances. Books are inclusive. They exclude no one. I'm going to show you in a minute how that changes the world. I travel around doing leadership meetings with the great Jim Rowan, and I hope you've listened to him or seen him online, but he said, "If you can read and don't, you're no better than somebody who can't." I want you to read positive, self-help action stuff like Raymond and I write, and all the 19 people on this thing write. You say, "Well, what did bookstore owners . . . " Bookstores are falling down again, and it breaks my heart.

**Mark Victor Hansen:**

When Jack and I go to the American Bookseller Association, bookstore owners and managers and distributors would come up to us, we'd sign all our books, and they said, "What you're doing, selling 15 million books a year is changing the world. People are coming in to get your book and then you buy five or six other books. You've kept us alive." I've helped millions of people. One Minute Millionaire, first line I wrote is, "I want to create a million millionaires. That's a trillion dollars." Well, now we've got to create a whole lot more to pay off all this debt." You say, "Well, can everybody read?" Four billion people are coming online right now. There's another guy I'd like you to look at, who wrote BODL, and wrote Abundance and wrote The Future is Faster Than You Think. Dr. Peter Diamandis, who's an MD from Harvard, a PhD from MIT, started Singularity University, is the smartest guy now on the planet.

**Mark Victor Hansen:**

My teacher Bucky Fuller was, but now it's Dr. Ray Kurzweil. Anyhow, I started the X prize with no money, but he wrote about it. Elon Musk gives them the money. They go to Kenya. They all go to 40 villages, and with a cheap $15 smartphone, they taught all the kids to read Swahili and English in a year and a half, and he got the $10 million prize. The point is that's fundamentally going to advance education, innovation, technology, culture in the world. What it does, it's just going to create abundance and now people are going to be able to do something [inaudible 00:23:46]. I hear somebody else talking. Oops. Am I getting feedback Raymond.

**Raymond Aaron:**

You sound fabulous. Keep going.

**Mark Victor Hansen:**

Okay. I just suddenly thought maybe you were trying to ask a question or something. Can books become an enterprise and a business? Well heck yeah. I worked at Dale Carnegie when I started speaking long ago. The books were amazing, because he he's been in debt since 1955, and his company makes $50 million a year or so. I hope you read How to Win Friends and Influence People, because while we're temporarily socially shut down and you can no longer shake hands, you can no longer hug, which Jack and I and Raymond have talked forever, now you got to do elbow bumps and foot bumps, we still need to stay connected. We still have high social needs, and books are a way to do that.

**Mark Victor Hansen:**

They're such a magnificent force multiplier to get your messages out. There's nothing better to give you credibility in the marketplace. I wrote a book on how to do books, called You Have a Book in You, which you can see if you go to receiption@markvictorhansen.com. You say, "Well, show me an example of something that really worked." Well, my hero is Abe Lincoln when I grew up in the state of Illinois. He read Harriet Beecher Stowe's Uncle Tom's Cabin. He was such a visionary leader. He read that, understood oppression and slavery was wrong. He wrote the emancipation proclamation because one book, one idea went in and he came out.

**Mark Victor Hansen:**

I'm telling you, freedom is expanding everywhere. I want freedom for 100% of humanity. I promise you, I am opposed to socialism and I'm absolutely opposed to communism. If you really know what's going on in places like China and that, they want to thwart the world. They got a million slaves there. It's tough. You say, "Well, what is the time that we're really in?" Well, one of the many great lines my teacher, Dr. Bucky Fuller wrote was, "Emergency causes emergence." Now, we individually and collectively come through an emergency called a pandemic, and we're still in it sort of. It's probably scared us, slowed us down, burdened us with fear and worries, and they're untold, no question about it.

**Mark Victor Hansen:**

The cliche and self-help action industry though, that you'll hear throughout these seminars I believe, it's not what happens to us, it's how we react and respond to it. I'm not making light of that because that's it. How are you going to react and respond? That's why I am so proud of you. If I were with you, I'd say, "Put your hand over your shoulder. Congratulate yourself for being at this seminar," because you've got to have courage, which means bravery of heart. We are all going to have to confront what stifled us, what stopped us, and it's going to be our time now to outperform yourself in love, outperform yourself in work, life, relationships, and your spiritual growth, and choose to outperform yourself totally and absolutely.

**Mark Victor Hansen:**

Because each of us have seeds of greatness deep inside, and it's adversity that you got to turn into an advantage. That's individually and collectively. Every one of us is filled with great riches, inner riches, wonderful, inner gifts that require a decision of a white-hot burning desire to release them, and be passionately on purpose about fulfilling your individual destiny. My destiny is to sell a billion books, and I'm going to do it. Crystal, my beloved wife and I discovered that when we wrote Ask and we interviewed, unequivocally the best people.

**Mark Victor Hansen:**

I promised you I'd do this story that is a very Chicken Soup story and I think you will like it a lot. Some of you know the story of Jim Stovall. He's 19 years old. He is a superstar athlete. He wants to be an NFL player. He gets recruited. He goes into doctor, checks him out, and says, "Kid, I'm sorry I got bad news. Six months from now, you're going to permanently and forever blind. You will never see again." Guys crushed. Now he was incarcerated in a 9x12 room. He's got a telephone. He's got a television and a radio, and that's it. He's complaining. His parents say, "Jimmy, you go down to the blind meeting." He goes there and they're all doing the same complaining, so that didn't do him any good.

**Mark Victor Hansen:**

Sits next to a blind woman who's a court stenographer, and he said, "I used to love watch [inaudible 00:27:51] on TV and see somebody throw away hook, but I can't see that anymore. Somebody ought to do something about it." I said, "Each one of us has got to decide what problem we're going to fix. That's the critical crux to what I'm saying, how to be up in down times. Decide what your going not fix and change. She said to Jim Stovall, "Why can't we do it?" He went? "Why can't we do it?" They created narrative TV. Now, if you're sighted, you don't even know narrative TV, but 14 million people around the world watch narrative TV about throwing a hook or child's grilling away. Cool thing is, we put Jim in our book *Ask, The Bridge From Your Dreams to Your Destiny*, because not only did he help the blind with that, but then he wrote a book called the Ultimate Gift.

**Mark Victor Hansen:**

I was selling 15 million books a year. Charlie "Tremendous" Jones said, "You got to write the board an endorsement." I read it, I loved it. I could see it. I wrote, "This should be a movie." He made a hundred million with his movie. The last line he wrote from a guy coming out of adversity through phenomenal destiny advantage. He said, "I now write books, but I can't read. I now make movies that I can't see." Ladies and gentlemen, you're about to be able to see stuff that you couldn't see before you came to Will Prosper Summit, thanks to Raymond. If we were all live, I'd say give him a standing ovation for being wise enough, wonderful enough, informed enough, enlightened enough to intrigue all of us to participant with him, and have you had the best mind awakening for prosperity ever in history.

**Raymond Aaron:**

Mark Victor Hansen, you did exactly what you promised to do. You were genius. You uplifted my spirit and the spirit of thousands and thousands of people who were listening. Thank you. You did a great job. You are the willow and not the oak tree. You are a genius. You are brilliant. I love you. I love you even more than ever. You and I have written two books together. Maybe-

**Mark Victor Hansen:**

Sorry, I gave you one extra. Maybe we got one in the future.

**Raymond Aaron:**

No problem. Okay. Bye bye. Thank you so much, Mark Victor. Bye bye.

# Start & Grow an Online Business NOW in this New World Order

## Francis Ablola

**Raymond Aaron:**

Francis has been my techie genius, webmaster genius, online marketing genius, digital marketing genius. He is brilliant. I am so proud that he is working with me. He is the co-creator of the entire World Prosper Summit. He lives in Florida. We hardly ever touch him but we see him constantly by Zoom meeting and by conference call, and he is one of us even if he's not in our office because there's actually no one in our office right now. Francis, just before you come on, I want to say that several people said they had trouble on the GoToWebinar link. If you are having trouble on GoToWebinar because there's thousands of people on GoToWebinar right now, but on YouTube, it's working perfectly, and on my Facebook private group Get Real with Raymond, it is working perfectly. So if you are on GoToWebinar and you can hear me, may be I'm stuttering, if you can hear me on go to webinar and you're having trouble, go to YouTube or go to my closed Facebook group but you have to join first. Either one.

**Raymond Aaron:**

In the chat, Francis has listed it several times. So either find YouTube or the closed Facebook group and join it. If you are actually a personal friend of mine, if you're one of the 5,000, it's also streaming on my personal Facebook timeline. There's lots of ways to get outside of GoToWebinar and Francis will be fixing that. Also there is a contest to see who can share the most, because if you share five to 10 people, you become a VIP automatically and there'll be gifts today and tomorrow which only VIPs will get, and whoever shares the most wins a prize worth 10,000 US dollars and the contest ends tomorrow morning, so you can still keep sharing today, and I love you. This is the biggest thing I've ever done. I've spent 37 years knowing how to get my tooshie on an airplane and go into a hotel bedroom and sleep overnight and then speak in a hotel meeting room, and now it's gone, so I'm reinventing myself as an internet marketer and the first thing I've ever done, thankfully with Francis's collaboration, is the biggest thing I've ever, ever done.

**Raymond Aaron:**

I've had a thousand people in Johannesburg, South Africa, I've had 540 people in Vancouver, Canada, there's tens of thousands of people who've signed up for this. It is the biggest thing I've ever, ever, ever done, and it's because of the collaboration with Francis, because of the internet, and because of wonderful people like Mark Victor Hansen and a total of 19 amazing speakers, including Francis Ablola. Take it away.

**Francis Ablola:**

Thank you, Raymond, and Mark was incredible. I am so honored and humbled to be here. This is an exciting, exciting event and I've been watching all the comments, I actually just took a picture. If you can see this, Raymond, this is my view right now. I have about one, two, three, four, five, six, seven, eight screens in front of me monitoring Facebook, monitoring YouTube, monitoring GoToWebinar and streaming right now, it's insane, it's incredible. Guys, I'm so excited to be here. I'm going to share my screen with you and I have a quick presentation that-

**Raymond Aaron:**

Here's my screen.

**Francis Ablola:**

Not as complex as mine.

**Raymond Aaron:**

No but I have two lamps glaring me in the face so that my face is illuminated and I've got this magnificent Buddha just keeping me calm.

**Francis Ablola:**

I love it, absolutely. As Raymond was saying, my name is Francis Ablola. I've had the honor and privilege to work with Raymond for over five years, I've known him close to 12 years now and it's been an incredible experience. Every time I learn from Raymond, I listen to Raymond, every time I talk to him, I learn something new. Every time I'm around these people, and one of the things, Mark mentioned Jim Rohn. Jim Rohn was a very early influence in my life as well. I had an opportunity to work in an event, my very first seminar I worked at was with

Jim Rohn and I've been a follower of his ever since I was 19. The biggest thing that I learned was stand guard at the fortress of your mind, and that's what this event is. It's standing guard at the fortress of your mind and being able to put the proper input in so you can have the proper output out, and that's what this event is.

**Francis Ablola:**

I only have a little bit of time so I'm going to go over some slides with you on, I call it "30 minutes of Awesomeness," and my job as an online marketer, I've been doing it for 15 years, is to share strategies that work to help grow businesses, and let's get into that now. Real quick bio, who is this guy? I've been doing this since 2001. I've helped lots of companies. Our company, Real Advisors is actually the number 281 fastest growing company in the country according to Inc magazine, maybe 500 last year. None of that's important, I have very little time. What is important is I'm sharing strategies that work with our market today, and I'll share what works especially now.

**Francis Ablola:**

If you are someone who is in business and you're struggling because of all that's going on in the world right now, if you're in your job and there's uncertainty there, if you've lost your job and you're looking for something else, if you're looking to belt skills, Jim Rohn would always say ideas and inspiration, he would start his events off by "I'm here to share ideas and inspiration." That's what I'm going to do in the next 30 minutes. I can't share everything but I can share some ideas and inspiration to help create a strategy and give you an action plan. Very quickly, it's about planting the seeds of growth, and if I can give you a seed and you can grow it into your own business, into something great, that's what I'm here for, and again, I'm so honored and humbled. We have a thousand people here, a thousand people there, all streaming everywhere to share some ideas with you.

**Francis Ablola:**

The virus has changed the way we internet, and this is from New York Times back in early April. Everyone's online right now. What that tells me, it presents a massive opportunity for everyone listening on this call right now. The internet has presented an opportunity right now that can reach more people, we can connect more people. This is one of the largest events I've ever had the honor, privilege of speaking at and I'm in my office in an empty room. I'm talking to people from all over the world right now and that's what gives us the ability, the internet gives us that ability to connect beyond just ourselves. So, so great, and again, things like Zoom, we're all on GoToMeeting right now. Google Classroom, they're soaring, and you have the ability to reach so many people in an instance. Amazing.

**Francis Ablola:**

Now, people are looking for leadership, they're looking for connection, and if you are a leader, if you have knowledge in your head or give access to someone with that knowledge in their head, this is the perfect time for you to get that in the world and make an impact on others. Hope that makes sense, and check this out. I'm a Facebook advertiser, I do a lot on Facebook advertising. Facebook advertising costs have decreased dramatically because lots of advertisers have pulled off. That gives us, the small guy, people just like you and me who may not have massive marketing budgets to be able to go online and actually share the message and reach their target audience very quickly. I can't speak on that all today, I'm short on time but I want to give you some ideas on how to approach that. It's about being reactive versus proactive to the crisis. I'll be honest, I have a confession to make. Actually, I'll get to that in a second.

## Francis Ablola:

Let's look at what's happening in the world today. 22 million in the United States, I know there's people from all around the world right now. 22 million people from the United States have lost their jobs, and that's a hard thing to look at. Businesses, people who've put their entire life savings on the line and risked it all to go into business are now hit with this massive thing, and that got me thinking, I was on a call with the Raymond Aaron group and we're having an executive call and we were just talking about all the people who are impacted negatively by this and the fact that we need to help. That's actually why we created the World Prospect Summit, it was from that conversation, we came up with the idea of what can we do to help as many people as possible, that's why it's a free event going on right now.

## Francis Ablola:

The bankruptcies, everything that's going on in the world, the financial world, and my business saw dramatic decrease in March. I want to show you our revenue from February 28th, this is one week. $154,000 from one week's revenue. Amazing, that was a good week for us. Let's look at April 3rd. $2,600. That is the same impact many, many business owners have seen. I will say because we made a difference, we made an impact, we changed it. Let me tell you about the story of Milton Hershey if you've never heard the story before. Milton Hershey, during the great depression, people stopped buying chocolate. The gross domestic product of the world I think dropped by 27%, unemployment was at 29%, the world was going in a very, very wrong turn and Milton Hershey who didn't want to see his life's legacy wasted went and got back into the business.

**Francis Ablola:**

It was like, "So people aren't paying money for candy. It's a luxury right now. What do I do?" Instead, he turned that product, the Hershey's with almonds, and was proactive, gave it a spin and said "For the cheap price of five cents, you can have more protein and more caloric value than anything else," and that product outsold more than he did any product in the history during that time, so it's about being proactive. I want to show you something else today. April 16th through 19th, we did a three-day event. my company did a three take three-day event. In three days, 160,000 collected cash from a strategy I'll share with you later today. Let me ask you in the questions box, is that something you want to learn more about? If so, let me know because we're going to share that with you. Great stuff, definitely a lot of opportunity. Thank you for sharing that.

**Francis Ablola:**

Moving forward, more people, again, looking for leadership, I said that early. People are buying online and I know people are buying, you are buying online. This is actually our orders from the recordings of this event. We've been getting, pouring in all day, people are buying online and you on this call are buying online. What would an extra $2,000 look like for you and your business right now? Would it be nice as a side income? Here it is. 200 sales at $10, 100 sales at $20, 20 sales at $100, four sales at $500, two sales at $1,000. When you break it down to the numbers, it's not very hard. It's actually pretty simple. I'm going to show you some ideas and strategies on how to get this. What about $10,000 a month? Would $10,000 a month be dramatic for you? I know for a lot of people, it would be. A thousand sales at $10. 10 sales at $1,000, one sale at 10,000.

**Francis Ablola:**

The internet gives us the opportunity to reach wide audiences, and if you have an idea of a product or service, we can reach it in an instant, for pennies to reach your audience and in tools like Facebook advertising. We'll talk about that here more in a moment. The big promise, I'm going to give you some tools you can use immediately in your life and your business right now to make a dramatic difference in your business, overcome some rope roadblocks, and build your brand at the same time. We'll talk about how to create raving fans and loyal clients in your business and also how to be seen and heard. Increase your profits, get more deals done, and how these things can be done fast, and I don't have too much more time. I'm going to run through these again. They're easy, they're simple, you don't have to overthink them. Some cheap and some are free. What works right now, these are the tools that I use in our business, that I use to get our message out in the world, so important.

**Francis Ablola:**

How to stand out? Here's the first tool. How to stand out with graphic design at a fraction of the cost. If you haven't used canva.com, it's a great tool. Canva, C-A-N-V-A.com instead of going the route of hiring professional graphic designers for things like magazines, posts and your social media and flyers. If you're on a tight budget and you're trying to get a message out in the world, canva.com allows you to create beautiful designs, very talented, very easy, very fast all through one platform, so that's canva.com. Another one, fiverr.com. I love Fiverr, F-I-V-E-R-R.com. It allows you to outsource things like graphic design, logo creation, website creation, basic tasks. Anything online that you're looking to create, Fiverr can do it for as little as $5. That's the name, fiverr.com. Great tool.

**Francis Ablola:**

99Designs, this is another design tool to help you stand out of the crowd and give you a better presence online. 99Design is a tool that lets you crowdsource your idea and create a beautiful end product from it. So you have hundreds of designers or thousands of designers from all over the world competing for your design and what they do is you put a product brief out and they'll come in and actually mock up designs for you and you get to choose the best one, and if you don't like any of them, you don't have to pay or if you like the very best, you can work with that person. Great tool. I know I'm going really fast, I'm checking out the comments here. I'll be happy to give you guys the slides of this presentation at the end and I'll show you how to get them, but there's a lot of great tools that we have, and again, if you are, we'll send you out the YouTube link, let me go and share that with you now.

**Francis Ablola:**

The YouTube and the Facebook groups are working really, really well, so if you're having a problem with GoToMeeting, check those out in YouTube. I put the YouTube link right in the chat box again. Happy to have you guys join us in those channels. How to make stunning landing pages super easy. This is one of the most important things that you can do because you need a presence on the web. ClickFunnels. ClickFunnels is one of the main tools I use. Actually, when you registered for World Prosper Summit, you were actually using a ClickFORM's platform, so you were using ClickFunnel's platform to access it. It's super simple, I think you can start with a 14 day trial. There is a $97 a month version, there's a $297 a month version, but if you have a business online, it's a great way to start. Again, this platform, this website, what we created for World Prosper Summit was right there on using ClickFunnels and we were able to generate thousands and thousands of leads in a matter of a week and a half or two weeks using the ClickFunnels platform.

**Francis Ablola:**

What about building raving fans? You got to have an email list right now. People are opening emails, they're interacting, the way you've heard about this login link was getting your email, so people are using email right now more than ever. Aweber. com is a great tool for that. If you've never used an email marketing list, build one right now. AWeber is the tool for that. Be seen and be heard. Be everywhere. Here's a trick, okay? We have super high-powered studios in our pocket right now, so creating Facebook lives, creating online videos, creating YouTube videos has never been easier than ever. Here's a trick, all right? Take a video and selfie of you watching this event right now and post it online and advertise it as your platform. "Hey, I'm spending my Friday and Saturday, I'm investing it in learning. What are you doing come check this out," and then you can tell them more about your business and things like that. Great tools. Content is King at the moment.

**Francis Ablola:**

GoAnimate. I love GoAnimate. What GoAnimate lets you do, it's a tool that lets you create cartoons, so if you don't want to be the face online, GoAnimate and will let you create cartoons. Do a voiceover, have someone do a voiceover, and for very inexpensively, create cartoons to promote your business and your brand online. Really, really cool. We use this all the time. Animoto let's use photos. Let's say you have photos and video clips, it creates amazingly professional slideshows for you to show and for you to get out of the world, to put on your social media and attract people to your business and to your audience. PowTunes. PowTunes is another tool. I actually helped a company grow from zero to $22 million in 18 months using PowToon videos as the landing page video. Think about that. It was a very, very simple explainer video, and again, there's a free version, there's a paid version. Great stuff. So many tools out there to help you expand your business online right now. Amazing, amazing, amazing.

**Francis Ablola:**

I'm getting some comments. I know I'm going fast so I'm going to show you guys how to get the slides to this presentation right after if that's helpful. If that's helpful, give me a yes in the chat box, give me a yes if you guys want these slides and I'll be happy to send them to you as well. VideoScribe is another one. This allows you to create those whiteboard explainer videos that look like this. They're beautifully done and VideoScribe lets you do this. It looks professionally done. Very low cost, very quick to do, you don't need a professional marketing team or design team to make that happen. I'm getting a bunch of yeses, thanks guys, that you want the slides. I know I'm going super fast and being cautious of time here but I want to give you as much value, and again, it's ideas and inspiration.

**Francis Ablola:**

Let's create reach. Nothing is going to work for you and your business unless you actually reach it and get out to so many people, right? So here's the first thing, UpViral. This program that you're on right now, this free event, we paid for a little bit of advertising and then we let viral marketing take place. UpViral is the thing that we use. When you shared your private link, when you're able to unlock, when you're able to share links again, UpViral tracked the entire thing. It was a beautiful tool to use, it's really inexpensive if you're not looking to grow. As you're looking to grow, you can grow with it, but really, really cool tool to get your reach expanded through viral marketing. Upviral.com. ClickFunnels and upviral.com are what we used to build this list here.

**Francis Ablola:**

BlogTalkRadio. Everyone can have their own blog and radio show right now. BlogTalkRadio is a great tool for that to allow you to increase your reach through channels that they've created. Anchor.fm. Any podcast is on here. If you're a podcaster, actually, if you're not a podcaster and you're new to it, Anchor.fm Lets you create a podcast in minutes and it makes it super easy, it's 100% free. Guys, I'm trying to eliminate any excuse that you have. Is it money, is it time, is it technology? Right now, never before has it been easier to reach your target audience and get to so many people so, so fast so easily with all of these tools, it's amazing.

**Francis Ablola:**

Livestream.com. LiveStream is another tool just like this where you can stream live events, and we've used this a lot to hold live seminars. This event that you're watching right now, it's on GoToMeeting but we can easily do it through a LiveStream, through a Zoom, something like that and reach people all around the world. There are thousands of people watching this right now on multiple channels and it's so amazing that it's made it so, so simple.

**Francis Ablola:**

How do you get found? Now it's important to get found, you need a couple of tools. Knowem.com, this allows you to leverage social media. Knowem.com is a tool that you enter once and it makes multiple social media profiles based off the information you give it, so get everywhere on the web. If somebody is searching on Twitter, on LinkedIn, on Blogger, whatever it may be, knowem.com is going to help you do that. Prlog.org and prweb.com, these are places both for creating press releases. To be able to release press releases out into the world. So you have a professionally written press release or I use a tool, I'm going to show you here in a moment, to create a press release and spread your message out there to everyone for everyone to see. Great, great tools, that's prlog.org, prweb.com.

**Francis Ablola:**

Content is king. Online, people are looking for messages. They don't want to be sold, sold, sold, they want to learn more about you, they want more information, so content is king. I'm going to share a few tools on that as well. Let's go to textbroker.com. TextBroker is an amazing tool that you can have writers from all over the US or all over the world, wherever you are, write content for you for as little as three, four, five cents a word. So if you're not a writer, you can have professional writers in any industry on any topic write for you as ghost writers and you keep that topic, it's all original. Amazing way to start building and become prolific in your market by sharing more and more information. Great, great tool there.

**Francis Ablola:**

Rev.com. I do this all the time, actually, write content for everything that we do. I have a 45 minute drive to my office, I live in the beach, I'm here in Jacksonville, Florida. I will turn on my audio recording on my phone and start dictating pages, start dictating emails, dictate everything I need and have someone send it to rev.com for me, there's actually an app to submit as well, and all of that's transcribed, so by that time later in the day, all of my material is already transcribed for me in an instant. Amazing way to create content.

**Francis Ablola:**

Now let's talk about creating your own products. Here's an idea. We're actually creating a product right now, so many of you have already bought the recordings of this event. The package will actually be sold again and again, and you can use that as DVDs and CDs if you want to, digital delivery, this whole thing is content that's valuable. Whatever you have, record yourself, make it content. Turn it into things that you can use. Zoom.us. We're using GoToMeeting right now, zoom.us is another tool a ton of people are using to create content. We do live virtual events from this. Virtual events are huge right now. This is the World Prosper Summit. You're on this now. We have thousands of people from all over the world tuning in. It's amazing.

**Francis Ablola:**

Actually, this is my martial arts school. My kids are young and they're in martial arts. They do now virtual karate school. My kids are on the path to have their black belts in less than a year right now and rather than waste an entire six months or a year and lose that momentum, we do virtual school right now, so think if you're a business owner, how do you do this? I have a friend who's a personal trainer. He can't go out and do personal training anymore. Nobody does virtual personal training. Think about being creative. How do you leverage this experience and the technology that I'm sharing with you right now to leverage in your own business?

**Francis Ablola:**

I told you about the strategy that we use for three days making $160,000 in our business when a few weeks before, it was $2,000 because of the crisis. We did a large virtual event and we sold a package, $12,000 package on that call to several people who were very interested. We had about 120 people on and we're able to create revenue in a live event which otherwise wouldn have had been canceled and we would have lost hundreds of thousands of dollars trying to put it in in flights, in time, in ticket sales, all of those things would have been lost if we had to cancel that event, but because we did it virtually, we were still able to make it profitable for us. I'll tell you about virtual events in a second.

**Francis Ablola:**

By the way, very important. I'm short on time. I'm doing a two hour masterclass for everyone on this call. April 30th, 2020 at 3:00 PM and go to worldprospersummit.com/virtual. Sign up for that class. You can actually open up a brand new window or sign up on your phone to join me on this two hour class. I'm speaking really fast because I only have five minutes left, but I want to be able to take time, I want to be able to answer all your questions, and I'll show you my exact model on how to make big virtual income from virtual events, the strategies that we do right now in our business. We've had one of the biggest weeks of our business using virtual events all online and everyone's learning so it's so valuable, so join me. It's worldprospersummit.com/virtual to join me on that 100% absolutely free event.

**Francis Ablola:**

Now kunaki.com is another tool if you wanted to make physical products. It's actually really cool. You upload your information and they make CDs and DVDs for you so you can add the physical products on demand for as little as $1.50 each. You can have them shipped out to people and they can pay that, buy that from you. Let's talk about selling products. Gumroad. com. If you're a digital creator, if you have content that you want to share to the world but you don't want to deal with the tech stuff and just want to get it out there, gumroad.com allows you to upload products to their system and sell it on their platform to their audiences and your audiences and you make the money from it. You pay them a small portion for their service obviously, but it's based off what you sell. It's never been easier to get your message out to the world and share with so many people and profit from it.

**Francis Ablola:**

Remember that chart I showed you. How many $10 products you need to reach to make $2,000 extra a month, $500 extra month, $10,000 a month and it's become so simple right now, you have no excuse. Samcart.com. This is the tool that we use in our business. We use it to make beautiful landing pages and sales pages, super easy to take orders online. You can actually take money using PayPal or Stripe which are both free services to take money. It's so, so easy to create products and sell right now. Let's talk about productivity. I only have a few more minutes left.

**Francis Ablola:**

Toggl.com. It's so easy right now to be stuck behind our computers and lost in the day. Toggl is an app for your phone or for your computer and you can track your time. If you're having trouble working from home right now, if you're having trouble staying productive because it's so easy to turn on Netflix, turn on Toggl. Work for a week and watch what you're doing.

Watch what you're doing and map your time out and you'll see where you're productive, where are you most. This is a great tool to track those things in your life. RescueTime, this is even more extreme. RescueTime actually sits on your computer and watches what you do and spits out a report at the end of the week or at the end of the day of what you did, where you spent your time, what you did online, and it gives you a report of how to use your time more effectively. So important especially if you're doing an online business, especially if you're creating a side income right now and you're looking for a way to do that.

**Francis Ablola:**

LastPass. I don't know how much time I've spent trying to find passwords and go back and go forth. LastPass actually saves you all that time and stores it in a secure server and lets you get the passwords out really, really fast. Outsource everything. A couple of minutes left. Upwork.com, one of my favorite outsourcing sites, we use outsourcing very heavily. We have about 50 people in our organization that worked with us. Several are in the Philippines, several here in Jacksonville, also in our Tampa office and around the world, but UpWork lets us find great talent all over the world for whatever we do, and especially in the Philippines. We have lots of Filipino VAs for very inexpensively in US dollars but still providing a great income for them overseas.

**Francis Ablola:**

Onlinejobs.ph is actually one of my favorite sources to find people as well, and hey, need a ninja? Some cool things. Fiverr. com, someone will dress up as a on Fiverr for you who'll also do a puppet show. Hopefully this was helpful. Again, I want to give some ideas and inspiration. That was very quick. If you want to get the slides, here's what you want to do. Go ahead and register for the virtual events and I will send you the slides in addition to joining me on the virtual events. Raymond, how'd I do?

**Raymond Aaron:**

You did amazing. You did seven hours of content in a half an hour.

**Francis Ablola:**

Short time.

**Raymond Aaron:**

Amazing. Go to worldprospersummit.com/virtual, you'll get two things. You'll get all his slides and you'll get an entire course for free. You'll get all his slides and you'll get an entire course for free. I'm so honored that you are our super genius, techie, webmaster, internet marketer, digital marketer, I'm so honored to collaborate with you, and you are a genius. All these websites, most of them free, that you've told us about are so powerful. Thank you.

**Francis Ablola:**

Thank you.

# Networking in the New Normal

## Dr. Ivan Misner

**Raymond Aaron:**

Ivan is such a gentleman, such a serious businessman, and yet he leads with his heart. He founded, many years ago, BNI, the largest networking and referral organization in the entire world. And the last two weeks, he's been working roughly 30 hours a day, trying to convert 9,500 clubs around the world, 9,500 clubs in the world, of 20 people each, in practically every country in the world onto Zoom instead of in hotel rooms. He's been busy. He has been forced into the virtual world. He knows an enormous amount about networking and his talk is networking in a lockdown. So the author of 24 books, my dear friend, a fellow member of a board that we're both on, a non-profit organization. I love him dearly. Here he is, Dr. Ivan Misner.

**Ivan Misner:**

Hey, thank you so much, Raymond. Am I able to pull up my screen for PowerPoint?

**Raymond Aaron:**

Yes. You just hit shares. I will send you the presenter slides now.

**Ivan Misner:**

No, I have my own set of slides. Are you able to give me the ability to share my screen? There we go. All right. Let's get started. So, Raymond, thank you so much. I'm going to talk a little bit about networking in the new normal. I'm guessing Raymond, you're able to see my screen now or my slides?

**Raymond Aaron:**

Yes, I can.

**Ivan Misner:**

Fantastic. You know what? We're all in this together. We are literally all in this together. The question is how are we going to respond to the challenges that we have right now? And I would argue that the best way to respond is through a couple of things that I'm going to talk about, a pouring into yourself, activating your network and innovation. These are the things that you need to do to be responding at this time. As Raymond mentioned, I am the founder of an organization called BNI.

**Raymond Aaron:**

Ivan, your sound just went away. If you clicked a button, please unclick it. Ivan, we love you. We want to hear you. Francis, take drastic action.

**Francis:**

Working on it right now.

**Raymond Aaron:**

Here we go. Yeah.

**Ivan Misner:**

Are you able to hear me?

**Raymond Aaron:**

Yes, we can hear you now.

**Ivan Misner:**

I saw that the audio connection was lost somehow. So, on 9,500 groups that meet in person every week. And so we had to figure out something to do. Otherwise, I would have seen 35 years of my business go up in viral smoke. One of the things that I think is really important is that I don't believe in this social distancing phrase, it's physical distancing that we need to be doing, not social distancing. In fact, you need to be more social than you have ever been before. This is about physical distancing, not social distancing. A recommendation, microdose your news, microdose the news. I see people who are just obsessed with what's going on in the news. I have one friend who is sitting in front of the news, flipping channels and watching it 10 hours a day and I'm here to tell you that that's the worst thing you can possibly do.

**Ivan Misner:**

Yeah, look, I believe you got to know what's going on in the world. So, we have an app, first thing in the morning, I check out the news to see what crazy thing is going on. Spend a few minutes before I go to bed, I'll take a look at the news again on my app, picking and choosing the things that I want to look at. Taking a look at positive news as well as negative news. But if you don't microdose the news right now, you're going to just see that the sky is falling. That is all [inaudible 00:04:17] And I'm here to tell you that if you don't focus on it, it's still going to find you, people are going to be negative around you. So, try to distance yourself from as much of the negative as possible. And don't sit idle, take action.

**Ivan Misner:**

What you need to be doing right now is looking for solutions, not obsessing about the problems. Raymond and I have a joint friend, Mark McKergow, Dr. Mark McKergow, who wrote a book called Solutions Focus. And one of the things that he talks about in that book is that if all you talk about are problems, if all you talk about are problems, you become an expert at problems. What you have to do is spend time looking for solutions. And I'll tell you a little more about what we've done to innovate and to find solutions in an organization that's been 35 years of meeting face-to-face, you've got to innovate right now. It's easy to throw a pity party for yourself. Look, I've done it. I've thrown pity parties for myself. And the truth is when it's over, I'm in the exact same place and I just feel worse. So no pity parties.

**Raymond Aaron:**

Ivan, your audio went out. What I'm going to do is actually stop sharing your webcam and that should help us with your connection. It seems to be the connection. Yeah. If you're listening to this and you can't hear Dr. Ivan Misner, just stay tuned. We're having a tiny technical difficulty. His sound will come back on in seconds.

**Ivan Misner:**

Oh, there we go. Can you see me now?

**Raymond Aaron:**

Yes, we can see you and hear you.

**Francis:**

I'm going to turn off your [crosstalk 00:06:37].

**Ivan Misner:**

Where did you lose me?

**Francis:**

It was about a minute ago.

**Raymond Aaron:**

The last thing you said was don't hold a pity party.

**Ivan Misner:**

All right, well, let's talk about that. Don't don't hold a pity party. So, there we go. Don't hold a pity party. I've held pity parties for myself and I'm here to tell you that at the end of it you feel worse and you're in the exact same place. No reason to hold pity parties. Have you lost me again, Raymond?

**Francis:**

We're still here.

**Raymond Aaron:**

No.

**Ivan Misner:**

Oh, there we go. You lost my camera.

**Francis:**

We're going to turn off the webcam, that might help the speed of your connection.

**Ivan Misner:**

Okay. There we go. I have a fast connection here. So I don't know what the problem is. Let me just bring this up. So forget the pity party thing. The truth is that we don't know what our future is, but I do know that we can influence our future. We can influence our future. And so the way to influence our future is to, I believe, build and work on your network. So the things that I'm going to talk about here for the next few minutes, you can find on a blog that I wrote on March 19th on ivanmeisner. com. So go to ivanmeisner.com and you'll find a blog that I wrote called Networking Online and the things I'm going to be talking about here for the next few minutes are all right there on that blog.

**Ivan Misner:**

The first thing that you need to do is activate your network. fear paralyzes people. I get that, fear paralyzes people, and you need to get past that fear. You need to let the fear provoke you. Provoke you to take action, to do things that you can do during this time. One of those things that you can do is to network. You can activate your network, connect with people that are in your network and innovate. These are things that you can do now. And you may be thinking, well, I'm in a business I can't innovate. Well, let me give you a couple of stories, true stories that I've just heard this week. One was a nutrition center that had to close down because the nutrition center was not a necessary business. And so she reached out to her network, she was a member of BNI and she reached out to her network and said, look, a lot of people want to make sure that their immune system is really built up. I have these immune packets, heavy vitamin C, if any of you want any, I'd be happy to ship them to you.

**Ivan Misner:**

And so, she immediately got about 50 orders of the packets, but the thing is one of the people who ordered packets told a big company about this, who then ordered 10,000 packets. She got the largest order of her professional career during the middle of the COVID virus lockdown. By the way, I don't like to call it a lockdown. I like to call it the great pause. I think it's important, as much as possible to frame things in as positive a way as you possibly can. That's really important. I hadn't planned on mentioning this, but when, Raymond knows I was diagnosed with cancer about eight years ago. One of the very first things that I did when I was diagnosed with cancer was I had a two hour drive to go meet my family down in San Diego and on the drive is the LA traffic, you're doing five miles an hour, I had a little notepad with me and I wrote down across the top, possible positive outcomes of a cancer diagnosis. And I came up with seven or eight different things that I thought could be a positive outcome. And I'm here to tell you, all of them came true.

**Ivan Misner:**

I wouldn't have guessed that as I was writing them down but I was trying to put myself in the right headspace to deal with a very serious issue. And they all came true. I would urge you to do the same, write down the possible positive outcomes of this great pause. And one of them is your ability to be able to activate your network. I used to have people who's say to me, I don't have time to network. You have plenty of time now to network. So spend some time networking and connecting with the network that you have. And so, I'm going to talk to you about the kinds of things that you want to do. Oh, let me give you one other story. Because I think this is an amazing story about somebody who activated her network. She was an upholstery shop.

**Ivan Misner:**

Now some of you may be thinking, yeah, I'm in a business, I can't do anything right now. She was in upholstery replacement shop. So, she would just replace upholstery on furniture. That was her business. It was completely closed down. So she thought, what can I do with all this fabric? Wait a minute, I can make masks. I can make masks, really high-quality masks. So she took this quality upholstery that she had, and she started making masks, dozens and dozens of masks. And then she put it out to her network. She said, I'm making masks. And people started showing up. They were six foot distance. They were physically distant but they'd have these boxes of masks. People would pick them up, pay for them. This one nurse wrote her and said, OMG, these are the best masks I have ever used in my entire career. I'm going to take samples of them to the hospital. I'm going to take samples of them to the nurses' association, to the hospice. And I think they'll place orders. And they have.

**Ivan Misner:**

She's now in the mask production business, probably not forever, but she said, I can keep my door open. I can keep my doors open. I can keep a couple of my people employed, the business is going to stay vital. Activate your network. She reached out to her friends and associates in her network and innovated and is going to make it through this virus. Do online face-to-face meetings. I'm sure a number of people have been talking about this. And it's really important that you get face-to-face, not just by phone, but actually see the person you're talking to and have a one-to-one. Now look, I'm the guy that started the world's largest in-person networking organization.

I still think face-to-face is the most powerful way to connect. But when you don't have that as an option, then this is a great opportunity for you to be able to at least look people in the eye and have a conversation with them about how they're doing what they're doing.

**Ivan Misner:**

And so, let's talk about what are the kinds of things that you should discuss when you do connect with someone on Zoom or Facebook, or I'm sorry, Zoom or LinkedIn or Skype. First thing you want to do is ask, how are you doing? How are things going? How's the family, everybody healthy? And then do a normal one-to-one that you would do. Start by asking, how are you weathering the storm? Have you been thinking about what you're going to do when we're let free from the great pause? Do you have a plan? Have you been thinking about it? Is there anything I can do to help you with it? Talk to them about what your plan is, maybe whatever innovation that you've done. Now, the kinds of conversations that you have will vary depending on the relationship that you have with the person that you're talking to.

**Ivan Misner:**

The foundation of everything I teach is these three words, I call it the VCP process. It stands for visibility, credibility, profitability. Visibility is where people know who you are and they know what you do. Credibility is where people know who you are, what you do, and they know you're good at it. And profitability is where you actually have a referral relationship with somebody. Now, I mentioned this because the conversation that you have with people will vary when you're having that face-to-face meeting, depending on where you stand in VCP. So my advice to you is start with the people that you're a profitability with.

These are people that are referring business to you. It'll be a very limited number of people possibly. The people who are regularly referring business to you and the people that you're regularly referring business to, reach out to them and have that conversation with, what's your plan? What are you doing? Here's what I'm doing. You can get right to the heart of the issue with these people.

**Ivan Misner:**

Then at credibility, you can do something very, very similar. You can get pretty close to the heart of the issue of the people that you are credibility with. At visibility, once you've gone through everyone on your list that you think you're at profitability with, everyone on your list, that you think you're a credibility with, then start moving to visibility. Do something. Don't just watch the news. Do something. So, at the people of visibility, what you want to do is connect with people that you have met that you know but you don't have a really good relationship with and start from there and say, hey, we have a lot of downtown right now. Let's get to know each other a little bit better. Let's talk, I'd like to learn more about your business so that when we're out of the great pause, we can possibly do business together or refer each other.

**Ivan Misner:**

One of the things that is very important that you want to do is ask them, how can I help you? And usually at the end of the conversation, this is where, what can I do for you? How can I help you in some way? Now I was doing a live radio show not long ago and the radio talk show host said, yeah, that's that old tired phrase, that doesn't work. And I said, no, we're on air still. And I said, well, actually I think it works very well, you don't have to use that expression, you can use a different expression but find out how you can help them. And he said, yeah, yeah, that doesn't work. So I didn't want to argue with them on air. Then we got off of air and we were talking and he was a good interview host, very good. And so, as we were talking off air, I said to him, hey, you do a great job on an interview. What other categories, what other areas of business are you looking for to do interviews with?

**Ivan Misner:**

And he told me some of the categories, and I told him a couple of names that were friends of mine that would fit the categories he was looking for. And I said, I know this guy and this guy, would they be good candidates for you to be on your show? And he's like, oh my goodness, you know those guys? Yeah, that would be fantastic, would you introduce me? I said, yeah, I'd be happy to introduce you. So I reached out to the two of them, they both got back to me the same day. They said, yes, they would love to be on his show. I reached out to him probably within three hours and said, they both responded, they both said, yes, here's their email addresses, you can contact them directly, they're expecting your email. He wrote me back. And he said, thank you so much, I really, really appreciate that, these are going to be great interviews. And I wrote back and said, and this is another way you can say, how can I help you? And he wrote me back one last time with one word, he said, touché.

**Ivan Misner:**

I wrote them back again and I said, no, it's not touché. It's walking the talk and, and how can I help you is really, really powerful. You may use it in a different way. I said, who you looking for? But it's the same thing. And he absolutely agreed. When you're doing a one-to-one, particularly with the people that you're at profitability and credibility with, and really, even more at credibility, where you want to go deeper and really want to get to know them. Use a technique that I call the gains exchange. It's called the gains exchange. It stands for goals, accomplishments, interests, networks, and skills. This is a great technique. Now, you can just write these four things down. However, you can find them in a book I wrote called Networking Like a Pro on page 58. If you happen to be in BNI, BNI has the form for this, but you just write these things down. Goals, accomplishments, interests, networks, and skills. Why is this important? It's important because what you want to look for are overlapping areas of interest.

**Ivan Misner:**

And when you find overlapping areas of interest with somebody else, it's much easier to create a relationship and a connection with that person. Much easier. Let me give you an example. When I first tried this out, I used it in a BNI chapter where we did this little workshop in there and I had them do this and I had these two gentlemen who did the gains exchange and they started doing it and one of them raised their hands, I went over, he said, look, we don't want to do this. I said, why? He said, because it's weenie. It's weenie? Yeah, it's silly, what are we going to get out of this? I said, do me a favor, just do it. Tell him what your goals are, your accomplishments, what your interests, what your networks, what your skills are. He'll do the same for you and when it's all done, I'm going to give you a little form to fill out and, on the form, if you don't think it works out, just say it was weenie, it wasn't worth it. He said, okay, fine. I'll do that.

**Ivan Misner:**

So, they started talking. They never got past interests in talking to each other. They would share each other's goals, each other's accomplishments, they got to interests, boom, full stop, never got any further. Why? Because they found out they were both soccer coaches for their son's soccer teams and the rest of the conversation was about coaching techniques and they agreed to scout for each other. These guys made an incredible connection and what was really amazing was, within just a few months, they started referring each other. How did that happen? That happened because they developed a relationship. And so, the idea with one-to-ones is not to close a sale, particularly right now, it's to make a connection and building a relationship. Networking's more about farming than it is about hunting. It's more about farming than it is about hunting. And that's what a one-to-one is about. Don't use networking as a digital in person face-to-face cold-calling technique. It's about relationship building.

**Ivan Misner:**

You can weather this storm. You really can. What you need to do right now is first pour into yourself. Now, to some extent, I'm singing to the choir because you're on this summit. And so you are pouring into yourself. That's important. Engage your network, reach out, make sure to activate it, go deep. If your network is a mile wide and an inch deep, it'll never be powerful. Go deep with your network. Connect with people, do one-to-ones right now, you will be in a much better position to come out of the great pause after this is over. If you've activated your network and poured into yourself, create a plan, innovate. If you have any interest, I wrote an article on entrepreneur.com in December of 2018. And in that article, I said, why the remote meetings of the future will be face-to-face and Raymond, you might find it interesting, I'm going to open it up for questions in just about three minutes here.

**Ivan Misner:**

You might find it interesting that at the transformational leadership council meeting that you and I were at in January, one of the things that I set for my big goal was getting the executive management team for BNI to recognize that within five to 10 years, technology is going to advance so far that it's going to be important that we hold BNI meetings, or at least have the ability to hold BNI meetings online. And my goal was to get them to that place mentally by the end of the year, the end of the year of this year, 2020, little did I recognize this COVID virus and that's exactly what we had to do and I'll talk about that in just a moment before I open it up for questions, actually I'll do it now.

**Ivan Misner:**

What was our innovation? Our innovation was to transition all 9,500 groups to BNI online. And we have successfully done that. We have literally 9,500 Zoom accounts all around the world, 70 countries. We run the same exact program except it's online. And we're having amazing success, incredible success. People who would have no business at all are generating business. People that are still struggling, at least have emotional support and people who are there helping them. All of our members have the opportunity to pour into themselves through BNI university and at least use this time wisely, rather than just wasting this time. If you wait until tough times are over, your business will be over. You cannot wait for the great pause to end. You must activate your network and innovate. These are things that you've got to do now, otherwise, you're going to come out of this and you're going to be like most of the population who spent their time in fear, instead of in focus.

**Ivan Misner:**

I believe hope is more powerful than fear. Hope is more powerful than fear. I had someone write to me when I posted something online and he said, why are you giving people false hope? Why are you giving false hope to people? And I'll tell you something, I don't think it's false hope. I think that hope plus action leaves fear in the dust. It takes hope and it takes action. And so, the things that I've talked about are both. You've got to have hope to have the right mindset and then you got to take action. And when you do both of those, it's not false hope. It's a plan for someone to get through challenging times. And I know for myself and for many other people I know, in some of our most challenging times, our biggest successes come out of it. And the previous speaker talked about that and I've had the same experience. So, hope plus action, it is absolutely more powerful than fear.

**Ivan Misner:**

Raymond, let me open it up and see if anyone's got any questions. I'm happy to answer questions now and if I'm able to turn my camera back on, I'm happy to do that.

**Raymond Aaron:**

Wow. You did a brilliant job and whilst Francis is looking for some interesting questions, I just want to say that I loved your presentation, I love how masterful you are and there's two quotes that I totally love microdose your news. Don't get swallowed up in the bad news.

**Ivan Misner:**

Yeah.

**Raymond Aaron:**

Microdose news. And so, I felt bad that I always check the news first thing in the morning, but you gave me permission to just microdose it.

**Ivan Misner:**

Yeah.

**Raymond Aaron:**

And I do. I just for a minute or two, just see if there's any catastrophe I should know about. And then I go back to my normal positive life. And the other is, it's not a lockdown, it's the great pause.

**Ivan Misner:**

Yes.

**Raymond Aaron:**

The great pause.

**Ivan Misner:**

And eventually, someone's going to hit play and we're going to go back out again. We'll either be prepared to go out or we will be completely devastated. I plan on being prepared and that's the reason why we didn't just wait for this to all end. We transitioned years in advance of what I thought we would do.

**Raymond Aaron:**

Well, I didn't prepare years in advance, but because of the collaboration with my co-creator, Francis, we have suddenly gone into this amazing world of The Internet. This is the biggest event I've ever, ever, ever hosted and I'm honored that you are a guest of mine and one of the very first guests.

**Ivan Misner:**

Oh my pleasure, Raymond. I couldn't imagine not being on for you. It was my pleasure to do it. I'm happy to answer any questions if somebody's got any.

**Francis:**

Yes. So we have been checking all three channels here. So on YouTube, we have the question from Fireproof. How do you elevate your network connections to be in it for an opportunity to come network a mentor? So how do you use your network to become mentors?

**Ivan Misner:**

To become-

**Francis:**

Mentor.

**Ivan Misner:**

Mentor. Well, listen, I'm glad you asked that question. That's a great question. As a matter of fact, I have something free for all of the viewers here today. If you go to Amazon.com, you can find a book there called The Networking Mentor, The Networking Mentor. It is on Amazon until midnight Pacific Time today for free as a digital download on Amazon.com. But you got to go to Amazon.com. So on amazon.com, it is free as a digital download, the book.

**Ivan Misner:**

So the question is, how do you become mentored? It really helps if you have a relationship of some kind with the person, or if you're introduced to the person by someone who has a good relationship with that individual. I have found that the best way to get someone to really mentor me is to find ways to help them first. If I can find a way to help them in some little way, then if I need help in some way, they're more than willing to do it. We have a fellow friend, Raymond, Alex Mandossian, and Alex, a TLC member, Alex kept reaching out to me for a period of time. And he kept saying, hey, what can I do? I've got an idea, we want to try this. And I'm like, I don't know if that's what I want to do, Alex.

**Ivan Misner:**

He said, no, no, no, I just want to help you. I just want to help you. And so he kept giving me these ideas and over and over and over again. And by the time he said to me, I need your help on something. He had poured into me so much that he said, I need your help with something and then I said, Alex, stop. The answer is yes. What is it that I'll be doing? And he said, you don't even know what it is. I said, it doesn't matter. You know me well enough. I don't think you're going to ask for anything that I wouldn't be able to do. And you have helped me so much. How could I say no? So, yes, what will I be doing? And he told me and it was easy and I was happy to do it. So the answer is try to help them in some small way and then it's easy for them to mentor you and then ask if they'll mentor you.

**Raymond Aaron:**

Ivan, that's your famous line, givers get.

**Ivan Misner:**

Givers gain, that's right.

**Raymond Aaron:**

Gain.

**Ivan Misner:**

Givers gain. Yeah. Well, I think my time's up. I don't know if there's time for another question but.

**Raymond Aaron:**

No, we're keeping ruthlessly on track on track.

**Ivan Misner:**

Ruthlessly on track. Raymond, thanks for inviting me. Francis, nice to see you.

**Francis:**

Thank you.

**Raymond Aaron:**

We will have a hug whenever we're allowed to.

**Ivan Misner:**

All right. Be well.

**Raymond Aaron:**

Thank you. Bye, bye.

**Ivan Misner:**

Bye.

# Write a Book While You're Sitting at Home

## Raymond Aaron

**Raymond Aaron:**

So, I'm going to talk to you about how to attain your biggest goals in times of crisis, and here we go. How much do you earn? You probably don't earn as much as you want to, and especially during this pause. So, are you ready for a huge change? Do you want to be in the top 1%? Well, the top 1% in the developed world is $300,000, 300,000 US dollars. You can create it with your creativity. Stop having blinders. Stop thinking you can only do what you're currently doing.

**Raymond Aaron:**

This pause has caused lots of people to be creative. You might say, "Okay, big shot, how much do you earn?" I won't tell you how much I earn per year, but I will tell you that the greatest experience I ever had was earning $1 million in a 90-minute speech. Wow. If you are not creative, life will seem unfair to you. So, you need to be creative, especially in times like now.

**Raymond Aaron:**

You must climb the 4-rung ladder of wealth. The first rung, as Dr. Ivan Meisner has just told you just minutes ago, is visibility. Every single person who earns more than you is more visible than you. And then as Ivan Meisner just taught you, every single person who earns more than you has more credibility than you. When you have visibility and credibility, you cannot stop the wealth from coming in. You cannot stop the wealth from coming in. I promise you four rungs, I've delivered three because the other one is in the wrong direction. It's in the dark side. It's invisibility, 97% of people in the Western world are completely invisible. That's why your life is tough, 97%. Where do you earn more money? At the top. You typically have to take one step at a time.

**Raymond Aaron:**

However, I've invented the only two-step, which takes you from invisibility and that's where 97% of my listeners are, takes you from invisibility and gobbles up visibility and credibility all at once because it's the two-step. But you already know that if you have visibility and credibility, you cannot stop the wealth from coming in. It's the most brilliant idea I've ever come up with. You must have your own book. You must have your own book. Mark Victor Hansen talked about having your own book. Francis Ablola talked about having your own book. Ivan Meisner has written 24 books. You must have your own book if you have any desire, any real sincere desire to create wealth for yourself.

**Raymond Aaron:**

I asked my dear friend Dr. John Gray who wrote *Men Are From Mars, Women Are From Venus, Kids Are From Hell*. Oh my gosh, it's hard to tell a joke when I can't hear any reaction. Please type "Haha" in the chat. Please type "Hahaha." So, I don't tell the joke and get a dead silence. Thank you. Oh, the "hahas" are coming in. Good, thank you very much. I asked John, if he could change one thing in his amazing life, what would it be? He shockingly said, "I'd rather have a book than a PhD." I said, "What are you talking about?" He said, "Call up a radio station and say, 'I have a PhD. Do you want to interview me?' No. No, they don't. But call up a radio station and say, 'I wrote the book on men-women relationships." "Oh my gosh, of course, we'd love you."

**Raymond Aaron:**

I wrote the book on real estate. I wrote the book on Bitcoins. I wrote the book on sex. I wrote the book on Pilates. I wrote the book on becoming a butcher. I wrote the book on flying an airplane. Whatever your shtick is, whatever your shtick is, when you write a book on it, you're seen as the person of giant credibility. Having a book means you can indeed aim higher. Yes, you can aim higher. Money will come to you. Opportunities will come to you. Income will come to you. Media appearances, patients, clients, joy, money, of all kinds will come to you when you have a book. I'm going to tell you what my life was like before a book. I'm going to tell you the one thing that I changed, and then I'm going to tell you my life now. So, here is my life before a book.

**Raymond Aaron:**

When I was born, I was broke. Maybe some of you have had that same experience. Then I took a job I didn't particularly like, and as a result, I got addicted to a substance and that substance was food. I got very, very, very fat. I'm a short guy, five feet, five and a half inches, and I weighed 212 pounds. I couldn't even bend over and tie my own shoes. Because I was so obese and because I didn't like my job, I didn't do a good job. My boss noticed it and he fired me. I went home and told my wife that I got fired. She did the only thing a reasonable woman could do. She dumped me and I learned something. I learned getting fired and divorced on exactly the same day are just extreme forms of market research.

**Raymond Aaron:**

What the marketplace was telling was nutritionally, I was overweight. Vocationally, I was fired. Matrimonially, I was dumped, and I haven't even told you the bad news yet. I was depressed. I was a 39-year-old life loser, $100,000 in debt. A 39-year-old life loser, $100,000 in debt. That's when the turning point of my life game, I decided to write a book. Now I was dead broke, but I had made a lot of money in real estate. So, I wondered what should I write a book on? Should I write this book How to Become A 39-Year-Old Life Loser: Seven Proven Techniques. I had the information to write that, but it's not the brand I was going for. That was just a joke, but here is the book I actually wrote, You Can Make A Million in Canadian Real Estate.

**Raymond Aaron:**

I was broke at the time because I lost it all in the divorce, but I still knew how to make a lot of money. I showed it to my mother. I thought my mother would be proud of me, "Ma, I wrote a book." She said, "Why do you have a broken picket fence across the bottom?" I said "Ma, those are houses. I drew them myself." She said, "Son, you could have drawn better houses when you were four." Nevertheless, the next 10 seconds of what I'm going to say to you is the most important 10 seconds of this entire presentation. If I bumped into you on the street

20 years from now, the next 10 seconds are the only 10 seconds of this presentation that you'll remember.

**Raymond Aaron:**

Get ready for this from age 39 to age 40, after having published this book, I got out of $100,000 of debt, the first time I was out of debt in my entire adult life. And then in one more year, from age 40 to age 41, I became a millionaire and I've never looked back. Wow, wow, wow. Even more impressive, my clients are getting there faster than me. Even more impressive, my clients are getting there faster than me. What is the one thing that I changed? Writing a book. That is the only thing I changed. Come into my life now. My dearest friend is Jack Canfield. We're on a board of directors together. We've written two books together. One of them in New York Times Top 10 Best Sellers, and we're currently writing yet another book together. Here I am on vacation with him on a cruise ship. He's a dear, dear friend.

**Raymond Aaron:**

This is an embarrassing picture. I'm not even sure if you can see me in this picture. That is the famous Tony Robbins, Les Brown, a dear friend of mine, Oprah's boyfriend, Stedman Graham. With this picture seems to indicate is that even for Oprah, size matters. When I took this picture, I was so embarrassed. I said, "Look, Stedman. Can I get another picture?" He said, "Sure." So, I ran around the entire hotel to find a stool, and I took a picture with me standing on a stool, but it didn't work. He's still taller than me even when I'm standing on a stool. Very, very embarrassing. Rudy Giuliani, the greatest mayor of all time. Bob Proctor, the grandfather of the entire Personal Growth Industry.

**Raymond Aaron:**

By the way, have you noticed that every single time I introduce you to a friend of mine, books drop down? Have you noticed when you go to visit a friend of yours, books don't drop down? Books don't drop down. Have you noticed that my friends earn way more than they think is reasonable? You and your friends earn way less than you think you deserve. The difference is a book. Sir Richard Branson himself. Brian Tracy, The Laws of Business Success. Brian Mulroney, the Prime Minister of Canada. Steve Wozniak, Dr. John Gray, Bill Clinton, Arnold Schwarzenegger, Robert Kiyosaki, the greatest wealth teacher of all time. These are all dear friends of mine. Best of all, you'll love this one, Shrek. Even Shrek has a book.

**Raymond Aaron:**

So, it's not what you know and it's not who you know, it's who knows you. Did these world-famous celebrities know me when I was 39? No. Did they want to know me when I was 39? No. Do they know me now? Yes, they know me now. I'm on their speed dial. They're on my speed dial. We are actually dear friends, but there's two problems that you have to solve if you're considering writing a book. The first problem is the foreword scandal. Foreword is not a direction, forward versus backward. It is a one-page letter at the beginning of a book, telling the readers how wonderful you are and how wonderful the book is. Unfortunately, celebrities charge up to half a million dollars to write the foreword.

**Raymond Aaron:**

So, here's the deal. You have to have a foreword. You have to have a celebrity for the foreword, but you cannot pay for it. It's not illegal, but it's scummy. It's just not nice. The other problem is this. Never join any program unless the guru himself is willing to personally teach you in a follow-up workshop. Never join any program unless the guru himself is willing to personally teach you in a follow-up workshop, critically important. So, how do you know when you're branded? Because branding is the key to gigantic wealth. When someone says, "Wow," about you, you're branded. When someone says, "Wow," about you, you're branded.

**Raymond Aaron:**

So, let's talk about branding. There are four ways to get branded, four ways. I'm going to teach you all four, you choose one. How many will I teach you? Four. How many will you choose? One. Here we go. Let's get started. Branding technique number four is branding by association, branding by association. When I showed you pictures of me with 100 of the most famous celebrities in the entire world, did your estimation of me, did your respect for me, did your credibility in me go up or down? Up. Did it go up a little or a lot? A lot. But you may not have worldwide famous author colleagues and so this just won't work for you, even though it's a great technique. So, let's go on to branding technique number three, branding by testimonial.

**Raymond Aaron:**

Now you might say, "Oh yes, I've got great testimonials," but maybe you don't when you hear my definition of testimonial. A testimonial cannot be from your client. What? Of course, the testimonial's from your client. No, a testimonial has to be from a world-famous celebrity. You see if you show me a testimonial that says, "Oh, thank you, you saved my life," and the person is Mary McGregor. Well, who's Mary McGregor? Maybe you made her up, maybe it's your cat, maybe it's your neighbor.

Maybe it's a homeless person. How do we know? But if it's from Gwyneth Paltrow, okay, then we know. So, if you don't have a world-famous celebrity doing the testimonial, it doesn't count. You've blown two, don't give up hope yet.

**Raymond Aaron:**

Here's the person who gave me a testimonial, the world-famous Robert Kiyosaki, who wrote the world-famous book Rich Dad, Poor Dad, but I like his second book better, Cashflow Quadrant. Here's what the amazing Robert Kiyosaki says about me. "I thank Raymond Aaron and his tapes on goal setting for helping me achieve more with a lot less stress." Wow, how do we know he said that? Because he wrote it on page 187 of his second book, in the first edition of his second book, page 187.

**Raymond Aaron:**

Here it is, "I thank Raymond Aaron and his tape on goal setting for helping to achieve more with a lot less stress." Wow, one of the biggest names in the world wrote one of the most amazing sentences in the world. That's a big deal. That's branding by testimonial. Because of that, I have earned $8 million, over $8 million in the last seven years because of that one sentence. I've earned over $8 million in the last seven years because of that one sentence. Wow, wow, wow.

**Raymond Aaron:**

But maybe you don't have great testimonials. Well, let's go on to number two, branding via achievement. Did you recently win a world record? Did you recently get a Nobel Peace Prize? Were you recently the mayor of your city, something like that? No. Well, let's see if I have any testimonial, any achievements. I've been in the who's who every single year for 37 years. For every single one of those consecutive 37 years, I've been on the very first page, but that's mostly for alphabetical reasons. I'm internationally syndicated on radio talk shows around the world. You can be on radio and television too, but only if you've written a book. Nobody wants you unless you've written a book.

**Raymond Aaron:**

Every single star of the movie The Secret had previously written a book. Every single person who ever gets on my stage for the last 37 years has written a book. You can't get onto anything big unless you have written a book. I'm sure you've heard of the movie The Secret, there were 40 teachers filmed for that movie, and I was one of them. Every single person who was filmed for the movie had written a book. Wow. Also, I bought and sold over 1,100 properties. That's over half a billion dollars of buying and selling in today's money. Those are a lot of achievements, but maybe you don't have any big achievements like that. You've blown three. There's only one left, you better qualify for this one. Otherwise, you can't get rich.

**Raymond Aaron:**

Here it is. Number one, branding by WOW. If you can do something or say something that people say, "Wow" to, you are branded. The easiest way to have somebody say, "Wow" to you is to simply say, "I wrote a book. I wrote a book." They will guarantee say, "Wow." It took me four years to write Chicken Soup for the Parent's Soul, and it hit New York Times Top 10. How much did I earn? Well, I get a royalty check every quarter. That means every three months, my first royalty check was $100,000. Can you make money with a book? Yes.

**Raymond Aaron:**

And then I wrote another Chicken Soup book for a smaller community, just Canadians, Chicken Soup for the Canadian Soul. It was the number one bestseller in Canada every single week for six months. My first royalty check was another $100,000. So, even in a much smaller community, I could still earn a lot of money in my very first royalty check. I've written another book, Branding Small Business for dummies, because I've been recognized by the For Dummies empire as one of the world's premier authorities on branding. How long did this book take? Well, I developed some new techniques, some new techniques that no one knows about. These are special new secret techniques.

**Raymond Aaron:**

I was able to write this book . . . Wait until the fireworks die down. I was able to write this book in 10 hours, in 10 hours because I use these secret techniques. Amazing. I wrote a book, I got rich. You want rich, write a book. It's as simple as that, but not in one to four years. The giant breakthrough is you can write a great book, really a great book in 10 hours. I have thousands of clients around the world from Singapore to Slovenia. Some of them take more than 10 hours, a lot of them take less than 10 hours. There's no race, there's no rush. If you want to take 20 hours, that's totally okay. The bottom line is you can write a really good book really fast. I know how to do it, as Lisa found out.

**Lisa Phillips:**

Hi everybody. I'm Lisa Phillips, author of the book, The Artistic Edge. I just wanted to share some amazing things that happened to me since my book was published. Within the first three months, I was published in The Washington Post three times. I was able to get a keynote speaking gig at the Tennessee Arts Commission, where my speaking fee was $5,000. I've had so many more incredible things happen from blog posts, conferences, articles, and also having my book being used as a teaching tool for school boards all across the US. So, thank you so much, Raymond, for encouraging me to write the book.

**Raymond Aaron:**

Wow, wow, wow. You have a book inside of you. It's way past time to get it out. It's time to make lots of money with a book, absolutely, as Jim found out.

**Jim:**

Hi. My names is Jim Hetherington. I wrote this book, Your Relationship Rescue Handbook in The 10-10-10 Program. Raymond says that it was going to change my life and it really has. Ever since I've written this book, I've been invited to co-author in other books. One is actually published already. I have my second book coming out in the spring. I've been invited to speak on stages. I've been invited to go radio shows and TV shows. I've been invited to go to trading events, where I teach.

**Jim:**

I'm on this stage of trading and encouraging other people. It just really has changed my life. I highly encourage you to get involved with The 10-10-10 Program. Write a book. Raymond's team is just amazing. Raymond himself is a great mentor, great teacher, has amazing systems that will really help you get this thing through, get it done, get it published, and get out of the sea of sameness.

**Raymond Aaron:**

Wow. Wow, that's all positive, but you probably have some excuses. So, let's talk about your excuses. "But I don't have the time." Excuse me, it's only 10 hours. According to Wikipedia, the average person in the Western world watches 11 hours of television a week. That means you could write 52 books this year and still watch your favorite TV show. "But I'm bad at English or English is my second language." It doesn't matter. Nobody sees your manuscript except your editor. Your editor sees it and your editors' job is to make your book look like an angel wrote it. Editing is needed, but it's not included in the program, because the cost is small. In any case, I teach you how you might be able to get it for free.

**Raymond Aaron:**

"Well, I've never written anything before." That's a good excuse. But of the several thousand people who have registered for my program, 95% have never written a book before and still using my amazing system, they've been able to finish writing a great book. "But I don't know what to write about." Well, this is where I come in. I'm a real genius at working with you, not just to help you write a book, but to help you write a book that makes you money. Other people can teach you how to write a book. You can just pull out a keyboard and type it yourself, but you won't make money at it. I teach you how to write a book that makes you money.

**Raymond Aaron:**

"But I'm just an employee." Then get ready for raises promotions and job offers. Why? Because no one in your entire company has ever written a book, who else are they going to promote? "But I'm a professional." Then get ready for clients coming in fast, because self-governing bodies for accountants and lawyers and doctors won't allow you to advertise or there's very strict restrictions on what you can do in advertising. But the absolute best advertising is your book and it's absolutely for free. "But I don't know much." You actually know much more than your readers. For example, I wrote the book, Double Your Income Doing What You Love, and so Richard Branson didn't read it. Why? Because he knows more than me, so what?

**Raymond Aaron:**

Tens of thousands of people got amazingly helped because of Double Your Income Doing What You Love, and so I help them. I help the people who knew less than me and that's the model of behavior for you. "What kind of books should I write?" Nonfiction if you want to earn the most amount of money, but you can also write a fiction, an autobiography, a poetry book, a children's book, a calendar, all kinds of books. I've published every single kind of book you could ever imagine. How much does it cost? Well, it costs as much as a small car. If you can't afford it, you'd better join. If you've been working for 5, 10, 20, 30 years, and you don't have a few thousand dollars to rub together, you better do something different. This is the most powerful something different you'll ever, ever get offered.

**Raymond Aaron:**

Oh, by the way, I'm not going to be offering this right now, but I just want to tell you what I'm very proud of. It's a six-audio program called the Ultimate Author's Marketing Guide. It teaches you exactly how to dramatically increase the number of books that you sell, but more importantly, it teaches you how the book can sell you. If you're salaried, how you can get promotions and raises. If you're in business, how the book will help you get way, way more businesses or business. So, I'm not selling that now, but people who get into my program a month or so later automatic, not automatically . . . But want to upgrade to that extra $3,000 Ultimate Author's Marketing Guide, because they want to sell more books and they want the book to sell them.

**Raymond Aaron:**

It's not available for sale. You'll buy it a couple months after if you get into my program. So, how will a book help you? I know exactly how a book will help you. You'll have lots of residual income and lots of free time, just like me and thousands of my clients around the world. Because of my books, I take a one-week vacation every single month. Here all the places that I have had one-week vacations at. I have 10 slides like this, but when I show all 10, people start drooling. So, I'm not going to show all 10. One-week vacation every month. I hear what you're saying. "I can't get away one week. I don't have that much money. My clients will leave me, my staff will be upset. My boss won't give me the time off." Yeah, when you have a book, I will teach you how to have a one-week vacation every single month like I do.

**Raymond Aaron:**

Even more amazing, I take a one-month vacation every year. You heard me, a one-month vacation every year. I slept on that beach in Fiji for a month. I went white-water canoeing in the High Arctic of Canada for a month. I went to the Rainforest in Ecuador for a month. I had a one-month honeymoon with my sweet wife, Karen, in the North and South Islands of New Zealand. For a month, I trekked to the Annapurna mountains of Nepal, for a month. I was in South Africa for a month. I did a double crossing of the Sahara Desert by jeep and camel for a month. I went all through Europe, actually in four months. From Israel, which actually was never in Europe, to England, which is now no longer in Europe, but for some reason I still call it my four-month European vacation.

**Raymond Aaron:**

I spent a month in Australia. I spent a month in Bali. I spent a month in Croatia. But my best, my all-time best, my sweetest, my most profound, my most memorable one-month vacation was Antarctica. Antarctica, what a glorious continent that is. There I took the best picture I've ever taken in my life. Do you want to see it? Here it is. Yes, that's me. I actually took my tuxedo to Antarctica. There I am standing beside a king penguin. Behind my head is not gravel, behind my head is 150,000 king penguins. I'm the one on the left. So, is my life the life that you want? I have no debt. I have very high income. I have very high wealth. I have the sweetest marriage any man could ever want. There she is. She's a very powerful CEO.

**Raymond Aaron:**

By the way, she's going to be on this show tomorrow talking about how you can earn an enormous amount of money being the CEO of your own company. She's also a competitive dancer, an actress, and a model, I'm honored to be in love with this sweet woman. Not only do I have the sexiest wife on the whole world, I also have the sexiest car in the whole world, a Tesla as it drives itself. When I click on the summon button, it comes towards me. Oh my gosh, it's a heartthrob. I also have a gorgeous new home, high residual income, and lots of time off to do what I want. That's what will happen to you. My program is called 10-10-10. You write a book of 10 chapters of your own words and I help you.

**Raymond Aaron:**

If you think you don't have enough wisdom, I help you do it . . . I've had kids as young as nine years old write a book. You actually have enough information. . . . in 10 hours, take more if you wish, that's not a race. But here's the amazing one, you'll be holding your finished, published physical book in your hand in only 10 weeks. I'm not talking about an e-book, which is good for lead generation as an internet marketer, but not for credibility. For credibility and branding it has to be a physical book. You'll be holding your physical book, your published physical book in your hands in only 10 weeks. Wow. I guarantee it. I guarantee it with an eight-point guarantee. I'm going to read you those guarantees right now.

**Raymond Aaron:**

Guarantee number one is about "I don't know what to write about." You may not, but I'm really brilliant at figuring out what you should write about, so that you'll make money with your book. You and I will work on the best topic, the best target audience, the best title, and the best subtitle for you so that you'll enjoy writing it. You'll get it out easily and you will make money.

**Raymond Aaron:**

Guarantee number two is even more important. It's the perfect book length. You see, if your book is too thick, people will shy away, and they won't want to read it because nobody's got time any longer. Even during this pause or lockdown, people don't think they have time. If the book is too thin, people will disregard it as just a marketing brochure. So, it can't be too thin, and it can't be too thick. It has to be the exact right length for you to get credibility.

**Raymond Aaron:**

Guarantee number three is about "When do I start making money?" Wait until you see this, this is the most shocking guarantee you'll ever, ever see. You start making money before you finish your book. You start making money before you finish your book. Indeed, most of my clients start making money before you start writing your book. Because I offer you a program to help you write a book that makes you money, but really, I teach two things. I teach how to write your book and how to make money from it really, really fast.

**Raymond Aaron:**

Guarantee number four has to do with "How will I learn how to write my book? How does this actually work?" The answer is I have created 19 videos and the videos are about 15 minutes long on average. You play the video and you do what the video says. In fact, after the first video, there's actually nothing to do. After the second video, it only takes one minute to do what I say in the video. Here's the shocking thing. You play the video, you do the work. You play the video, you do the work. Once you play the 19th video . . . Wait until you hear this. Once you play the 19th video, you are holding your book in your hand. Wow, wow, wow. That's my guarantee number four.

**Raymond Aaron:**

But you might say "Oh, Raymond, you're so positive. You're so positive, but my problem are so heavy." Well, the reason your problems are so heavy is you're drowning in the sea of sameness. The reason your problems are so heavy is you're not visible and you don't have credibility. The reason your problems are so heavy is you don't stand out in a crowd. You look the same as everybody else in your industry. You can go places you never imagined you can go when you follow me and write a book effortlessly that makes you lots of money.

**Raymond Aaron:**

So, what is guarantee number five about? It's about "How can I get a famous celebrity for my foreword?" You have to have a foreword. You have to have a famous celebrity write it for you, and you can't pay for it. So, how do you handle all that? Guarantee number five, I write the foreword for you. I will write the foreword for you. I am a famous celebrity. Here's a book that I published called The You-nique You. Below the author's name, it says, "Foreword by Raymond Aaron, New York Times bestselling author."

**Raymond Aaron:**

So, let me say a few things about this. Number one, if they know me, they'll say, "Well, foreword by Raymond Aaron." If they don't know me at all, they'll say, "Wow," because they'll say, "Foreword by New York Times bestselling author. Wow, how'd you get a New York Times Top 10 bestselling author to write the foreword for you?" By the way, if you already know somebody way more famous than me, use the person that you know. But for most people, they don't know any world-famous authors, celebrities. So, they're eager to use me on the cover of their book as their foreword.

**Raymond Aaron:**

Remember, you can get there faster than me. You can get there faster than me, because I didn't have anybody brilliant, helping me when I wrote my book many years ago. This is your opportunity to get a master helping you not just write a book, but helping you make money from that book, even before the book is out and even before you start. You can earn your annual income in one speech, but only if you've written a book. No one has ever gotten on my stage without writing a book. No one got into the movie The Secret without having previously written a book. You can't get on radio or television. It can't happen unless it's a tiny show.

**Raymond Aaron:**

Like if there's somebody that hardly anybody knows that the host is some little phony internet radio show, yeah, of course you'd get on those, but there's only nine people listening. It's hardly worth it. If you want to get on to a real radio or television show, if you want to get onto a real program that really brands you, you must have written a book.

**Raymond Aaron:**

Here's the hugest thing. Here is the totally hugest thing. It's about how can I get Raymond's personal help? I've helped thousands of people write their book, how can you get me personally? You might think, "Oh my gosh. I'll register for the program, but then I'll never see Raymond again." Wait until you hear this. You can get my personal help, because I personally conduct a workshop, a three-day Get Your Book Done workshop, a three-day Get Your Book Done workshop. I personally host it. There's a small group. You meet with me and I personally help you. Wow, wow, wow.

**Raymond Aaron:**

Next is how long do I have? Well, I already told you, 10 weeks. It takes 10 weeks to be holding your finished published book in your hand. But guarantee number seven is you get one full year, not just 10 weeks, one full year. However, somebody broke the 10 weeks and that was Chinmai Swamy, who wrote

Run Before You Walk in only 6 weeks. So, then the contest was on. People wrote their book in 5 weeks, 3 weeks, 1 week.

**Raymond Aaron:**

I figured, "Oh my gosh. One week, that's crazy. No one's going to write a book in less time than that." Until this teenage girl, this teenage girl at age 15 wrote #Success in 4 days from registering for my program to writing the entire book to getting it edited and formatted. Finding a publisher, getting it printed, having it sent to her home, opening the box, taking out the first book, and holding it up to her face, and texting a selfie to me in four days. Yes, amazing. If a 15-year-old teenage girl can do it, so can you. If a 15-year-old teenage girl has enough information and life experience to write a book, so do you.

**Raymond Aaron:**

And then the next guarantee is about "What will Raymond do if I write other books?" Wow. So, here is the very hugest, the very, very hugest, there is no risk to you whatsoever. There is no risk to you whatsoever. You can write as many books as you wish using my patented technology. There are eight guarantees and there's no risk to you whatsoever. You get all my information in the 19 home study videos, and you get all my information in the three-day Get Your Book Done workshop. You get all the 19 videos and you get also to be live with me in the Get Your Book Done workshop. I usually hold the Get Your Book Done workshop in Hawaii, because if I'm going to be somewhere, it might as well be Hawaii.

**Raymond Aaron:**

Now listen carefully. There are 31 secret marketing messages that have to be in your book. You've been thinking about putting content in your book. Well, of course, there has to be content in your book. But listen carefully, McDonald's produces a hamburger, is it the best hamburger in the world? No, it's a mediocre, even less than mediocre hamburger. The bun is dead. The patty is dry. You don't get any choice of condiments. The pickle that they put in is so thin you could read a book through it. Yet, it's the biggest selling burger in the world. Why? Because of the marketing, not because of the burger. Because of the Golden Arches, because of the Ronald McDonald clown, because of the playgrounds, because it advertises on kid's TV shows.

**Raymond Aaron:**

It's the marketing in your book that will get your book sold. It's the marketing in your book that will get the book to market. You must have 31 secret marketing messages in your book. If you don't, the world inventory of your book will sit collecting mildew in your garage. So, many people who write a book, the world inventory's in their garage. They boast to me, "No, it's selling. I sold nine copies so far in a few months." Like it just won't sell. You must have my secret marketing messages. They're mandatory. You might say, "No, no, I'll just read a book by myself." Don't you dare, because it won't turn out the way that you want.

**Raymond Aaron:**

But if you're still sitting there wondering, then here is the best news of all. It is time for a change. It's time to let the book do it for you. It's time for a giant discount. I told you it's a small car, but let me be really, really clear. It's 28,000 US dollars. It's 28,000 US dollars. But because you're on this World Prosper Summit, I will likely give you a discount. Stay tuned.

**Raymond Aaron:**

> Escape the sea of sameness. Climb up onto the island of individuality with a book, so that you can float effortlessly for the rest of your life down the river of relevant differentiation. You are unique and special, earning as if you're ordinary. You are unique and special, pretending that your ordinary. Stop being ordinary, you actually aren't ordinary. You are very special, but you're pretending that you're ordinary.

**Raymond Aaron:**

> If I lined you up with two other people in your industry and I asked a prospective client to choose one of them, they'd say, "I can't, they all look the same." If you look the same, you are the same. You'll earn what everyone else earns, which is far less than they should. The average person in the Western world dies broke, don't do what other people do. This is an unbelievably powerful testimonial from Emma, who wrote #Success in only four days. To prove it's a great book, watch this. This is an amazing totally true testimony.

**Emma:**

> Two years ago, when I was 15, I published my first book, #Success: How Teens Can Create Their Own Brilliant Future. Immediately after my book was published, I started getting wild results. I went to a new school and my book was already in the school library on display, right when you walk in. People had ordered my book, and reading it, and were coming up to me when I didn't even know them, and saying like, I had inspired them, and they were so proud of me. I was invited to all sorts of school activities right when I was a new student, because my brand was so high already from the book that I had written. The whole process was super easy, and it

was super quick. The program really, really works and it gets amazing results.

**Raymond Aaron:**

Wow, wow, wow, totally true story. So, here's the final, final, final, final discount. Why am I giving you a discount? Wait until you see this, because it's my birthday. I'm 75 years old. It's not exactly today that's my birthday, but it's close. It's around now. If you're not going to give me a gift on my birthday, then I'm going to have to give you a gift on my birthday. The gift is going to be thousands and thousands of US dollars discount. Before I tell you what the amazing discount is, I want to give you another testimonial which is genius. You see, you think you know what your price should be. You think you know what your salary should be.

**Raymond Aaron:**

You think you know, because if you're drowning in the sea of sameness, if you don't stand out, if you're not branded, you have to sell yourself at whatever everybody else is selling themself at. But Nathan wrote a book through my program. He does Snow removal in the City of Toronto, Canada, and snow removal for residential homes. To remove the snow from the sidewalk and from the driveway is $850. You go to anybody, they'll all remove your snow for the winter for $850 for the season, but Nathan is getting people running to him at 50% higher at $1,200. Because when you're branded, you can charge way more, and people will grab you. Watch this.

**Nathan:**

Some exciting news for you. Right now, I'm enrolling clients at a price that's higher than the competition. You heard it, higher.

It's all because of your lessons on branding. I mean, just the other day, I enrolled one client at $1,100. My competition last year charged them $850. This guy came running to me, enthusiastically signed up for $1,100 dollars. I mean, just today, I just wrote a new client for $1,200 dollars. Raymond, you're amazing. That's all I could say and just what Raymond says really works. I can't believe it. It's unbelievable.

**Raymond Aaron:**

Wow, wow, wow. I told you about the Get Your Book Done workshop, I usually hold it in Hawaii. Well, let me tell you the news, I'm holding it by Zoom. May 22, 23, 24, I'm holding it by Zoom. May 22, 23, 24, it's coming up in just a few weeks. If you've never used zoom, it's this wonderful, robust platform where you just click on a link, you just click on it, and suddenly you're in a room and your face shows with everyone else's. You're actually looking straight into the eyes of everybody in the room. It's actually more intimate than being there in person, because if you're in person, you only see the backs of the heads of the people in front of you. You don't even see the heads or the faces or anything of the people behind you and you have to turn to see the people beside you.

**Raymond Aaron:**

So, it's not that intimate. Weirdly, counter intuitively, Zoom is more intimate. We get more done, and the feedback forms are even better. You can attend from anywhere in the world. My Zoom classes are even more exciting. I get higher, and better, and more loving feedback from the virtual Get Your Book Done. It's amazing. May 22, 23, 24. I have something even more amazing for you. I'm holding a Zoom class every month, May, June, July, August. So, if you're not available in May, don't worry. You can attend it in June, and we'll be announcing the date. So, don't use that as your excuse for not registering because I'm holding it every month.

**Raymond Aaron:**

Here is my last video testimonial and it is the most shocking, Nick Bradley. He lives in England. He earned 50,000 British pounds sterling, £50,000 that's like 60,000 - 70,000 US dollars, 80,000 - 90,000 Canadian dollars. He earned 50,000 British pounds before his book was finished, and he earned it in one minute. in one sale. Unbelievable. Watch this true story.

**Nick Bradley:**

My name is Nick Bradley and I'm the award-winning author of Zero To Authentic Hero. Raymond Aaron showed me how to write the book and create a brand for myself. I spend a few thousand pounds doing that, but I wanted to get a good return on my investment. So, I wanted to make tens of thousands of pounds back on that time. I went to a conference and didn't even had a book. I hadn't even finished writing my book. So, I printed the cover and I wrapped it around my notebook. I held it up and I had one client who's paid me £50,000. That's even before I write the book. So, thank you, Raymond Aaron.

**Raymond Aaron:**

Wow, wow, wow. There's a strictly limited admission to my Get Your Book Done workshops even though it's by Zoom and even though I could have thousands of people there. I limit it because I want to be intimate. I want to be able to work with each person individually, so I keep them small, strictly limited admission. What you do is you enroll, I will give you the link very soon. Right after that, a coach will call you. Wow. So, it's 28,000 US dollars. Wait until you see what I have reduced it to.

Wait until you see it. Are you ready? Get your finger ready to click on the link. It'll be amazing. You won't believe it. Are you ready? Only 997 US dollars. Only 997, unbelievable! Reduced from $28,000.

**Raymond Aaron:**

Another gigantic bonus, my $3,000 Ultimate Author's Marketing Guide, I'm including that. Wow. Another thing . . . Wait until you see this. Register right now at OfferFromRaymond. com/Platinum, OfferFromRaymond.com/Platinum, OfferFrom Raymond.com/Platinum. There's nothing that I say that's as important as you're leaving immediately and typing that in or clicking on the link. My staff is putting it on the chat right now, so you can just click on it. Otherwise, you can just type it, OfferFromRaymond.com/Platinum.

**Raymond Aaron:**

Hold on. I've got something else to say, it is tax deductible against business income, because this expense helps you make more money. So, whatever the tax deduction is for you, it is less. There's no retail sales tax. Many provinces, many states, many countries have a retail sales tax. There is no retail sales tax for you, OfferFromRaymond.com/Platinum. I've got even a better news. Wait until you see this. I've created the greatest solution in the world. The only thing that's missing on the solution is you. It's only $997. US, but hold on. I have something amazing to tell you. Hold on, it's not US. Wait until you see, it's Canadian. $997 Canadian. That's another 35% discount. It's about 35% discount.

**Raymond Aaron:**

So, whether it's in Euro or US, whether you live in Euro land, or Swiss franc land, or British pound sterling land, or a US dollar land, wherever you live, it's about another 35% discount, because it's only Canadian dollars. Oh my gosh, it's unbelievable. I have never ever, ever, ever offered it at this rate. This is a spectacular discount, just for people on World Prosper Summit. It's unbelievable. I've never done this before. I am the only book writing teacher who makes sure that you make money with your book.

**Raymond Aaron:**

I'm the only book writing teacher who is himself, a New York Times bestselling author, and the only book writing teacher who has himself written a Chicken Soup book and a For Dummies book. I am the only book writing teacher who gives you an official launch. I'm the only book writing teacher who gives you 100% of your sales, not 6%, and on and on and on. If you need a payment plan, it's only two times $600 Canadian. It's only two times $600 Canadian. OfferFromRaymond.com/Platinum, OfferFromRaymond.com/Platinum. It's amazing and it's in Canadian dollars. There's so many things that I offer you. It's only two times $600. If you want a payment plan in Canadian dollars, there is my final offer, OfferFromRaymond.com/Platinum. It's only $997 Canadian to register for the entire program.

**Raymond Aaron:**

If you need a payment plan, it's only two times only $600 Canadian. If you have any questions whatsoever, just email MPatel@aaron.com, MPatel@aaron.com. Just go to OfferFromRaymond.com/Platinum. You'll see it in the chat, you can just click on it, or you can type it in yourself. Just type it in correctly, OfferFromRaymond.com/Platinum. It's only $997 Canadian which is I don't know if something like $600 or $700 US, €600 or €700 euros, £600- or £700-pounds sterling. It's just an enormous discount. If you need a payment plan, it's two times $600.

**Raymond Aaron:**

If you have an issue, if you can't get in or your card isn't working or you have to pay tomorrow or something, if you have any issue at all, or you want to wire us the money or whatever, just contact MPatel@aaron.com. He is my Chief Financial Officer. He is an accountant. He is very noble. He's very compassionate. He will listen to you. He will help you in any way possible. OfferFromRaymond.com/Platinum, OfferFromRaymond.com/Platinum. It's only $997, it's always US. I travel all around the world from Singapore to Slovenia. I always offer it in US dollars. This is the first time I've offered it in Canadian dollars online. It's unbelievable.

**Raymond Aaron:**

If you need a payment plan, it's too easy monthly installments of $600, where only $600 is due today. If you have any problem whatsoever, MPatel@aaron.com, MPatel@aaron.com. Francis, that's my show. I've ended 10 minutes early. Now is the time we could go live and answer people's questions. I would like to leave this on the screen and just hear your voice and my voice, if we can do that, Francis.

**Francis Ablola:**

Yes, absolutely. That was wonderful, Raymond. Great job. I'm getting a lot of great comments across the board on YouTube, on Facebook, and in the chat here.

**Raymond Aaron:**

Wow. So, we're on Facebook on my timeline. We're on Facebook on my private group, my closed group, Get Real With

Raymond. We're also on some other Facebook groups that I've shared it to. My wife has just shared it to her Facebook timeline. Many people are sharing it to their Facebook timeline. If you see it, just share it to your timeline. It's also on GoToWebinar. It's also on YouTube. It's everywhere. It's gone viral. I've never had tens of thousands of people register for any event I've ever done in my life. Oh my gosh, the internet is blowing up over this.

**Francis Ablola:**

We literally blew up GoToWebinar. We actually had so many people on, trying to log on at the same time. It caused issues on GoToWebinar. That's why we're on Facebook and YouTube. Amazing.

**Raymond Aaron:**

That's our very first speaker Mark Victor Hansen. Even though he's so wonderful, because he was the first speaker. Unfortunately, the problems happen on his half hour show where the screen froze, his audio cut out. It's not because of us. It's because GoToWebinar has never seen a webinar [inaudible 00:50:23] as this. They have never experienced it. My first online venture, thankfully, I'm collaborating with my wonderful, Francis Ablola, is such a knockout bestseller, bestseller. It's free for God's sakes. Wow, wow, wow, wow. So, do you have some questions?

**Francis Ablola:**

Yes. Anyone have any questions, go ahead and put them into the chats. Let's see. If you have any questions, go ahead and put them in the chat. We'll make sure to answer them. I'm looking for questions now. Everyone's just so amazed and shocked.

Okay, here we go. "I will start writing my book. Well, will you write the foreword for me?"

**Raymond Aaron:**

Yes, I'll write the foreword for you. I guaranteed it. I'll write the foreword for you.

**Francis Ablola:**

"I am 13 years old. Do you think I can still write my book?"

**Raymond Aaron:**

Excuse me, 13-year-old. Emma wrote #Success at 15, but my youngest is 9. It's a guy in the United States. So, a young boy in United States. He wrote the book on snakes. He knows eight snakes. It's a small book, but nevertheless, for the rest of his life, he can say, "I wrote a book at age nine, and it was published." Wow.

**Francis Ablola:**

Well, well, well, bye bye bye. Awesome. Let's see. I felt, [inaudible 00:51:50], like a nine-year-old. There are so many questions coming in from different channels. I'm trying to keep up. Let's see. "How do you help everyone who enrolls with these consultations, Raymond?"

**Raymond Aaron:**

First of all, I just want to say something. That $997 ,which is basically $1,000 is only 700 in US dollars, $1,000 Canadian is 706 US dollars. That is an unbelievable discount. That is a 30% discount from $997, which is almost $1,000. It's only 706 in US dollars. Wow, wow. It's crazy. That's a gigantic discount.

**Francis Ablola:**

Outstanding.

**Raymond Aaron:**

What was that question?

**Francis Ablola:**

Let's see, I lost that question. Let's see. Here's another one. "Will you help me publish it?"

**Raymond Aaron:**

I will show you exactly what you have to do to get it published. I'll take total care of you. It's only 650 in euro. Oh my god. It's only 650 in euro. This is crazy.

**Francis Ablola:**

Raymond, here's a question. "I've been through a lot in my life and now handicapped. Can you help me tell my story to the world?"

**Raymond Aaron:**

Oh my gosh, I would be honored to tell your story. There are many people who write a book about their adversity, about getting through cancer, about being handicapped, about getting wrapped up in a car accident, and they tell their story. It's so moving, and it sells a lot of copies. Yes, I would love to help you. It's an important book. I'd be honored to write the foreword for that book. In pound sterling, it's only 572. Oh my god. £572, hold on. I don't think I should have done this. That's way too low. Oh my God, that's way too low. Okay, so you better do this quickly because I'm not leaving it up for long. This is crazy. 572-pound sterling, oh my god.

**Francis Ablola:**

Raymond, someone has asked me if there's different dates other than the first one that you mentioned.

**Raymond Aaron:**

Yes, May 22, 23, 24. But because I keep the classroom size down, I'm holding another one in June, another one in July, another one in August. It's every month by Zoom. If you can't come in May, just come in June. But in any case, you'll immediately get the 19 videos that you can watch and start writing your book.

**Francis Ablola:**

Wonderful. "When do you start the training?"

**Raymond Aaron:**

I you want me to personally train you, if you want me to personally train you live, it's May 22, 23, 24 by Zoom. If you want to play the videos, you can start playing them tonight. You can start playing them today, because you'll immediately get told exactly what the password is to get into the videos. You can watch the videos and start writing your book today by watching my videos, or you can wait until May 22, 23, 24 and I will teach you personally. Now, the videos were done about a year ago, and there's been some technological improvements in book writing. So, you'll only find out the latest by coming to my Zoom class, May 22, 23, 24, or in June, or July, or August. Because I'm holding the Zoom class, Get Your Book Done, every month. If you have any issue-

**Francis Ablola:**

A lot of questions coming in from different channels here. "Do children's books do well?"

**Raymond Aaron:**

Oh my gosh. Yes. One of the books I wrote, Sharkey the Lonesome Sand Shark, Sharkey the Lonesome Sand Shark is selling like crazy. Sharkey the Lonesome Sand Shark is selling like crazy. I've published many, many children's books. I'll help you write a children's book if you wish, a children's book, an autobiography, a cookbook, a fiction and nonfiction, whatever you want. Now, if Francis does not read out your question, go to MPatel@aaron.com. You can see it on the bottom of your screen, MPatel@aaron.com. If you don't get your question answered right now by Francis and by me

**Francis Ablola:**

Do real estate books do well right now?

**Raymond Aaron:**

Oh my gosh. There is never a shortage of the need for real estate books. If you are a realtor, if you are a mortgage broker, if you are an appraiser, if you're a renovator, if you have anything to do with real estate, people always need real estate books. There are a million real estate books out there, but nobody cares. If you're talking to somebody and you're offering your service and they say, "Well, I've been thinking of using my sister as my realtor or the guy down the street as my realtor." All you have to do is say, "I wrote the book on real estate." "Oh my gosh, you wrote the book on real estate? Of course, I'll use you." It trumps anything and gets you into places you could never believe, and it gets you gigs. You will get gigs that you won't believe.

**Raymond Aaron:**

I remember I was at a RE/MAX party because I'm a RE/MAX realtor. I was speaking to two other realtors who were way, way better than me. I'd only been in one day. I just passed my exam. It was my first day as a realtor. They had been in for decades and really knew everything. A woman behind me said she's listing her home for sale. So, the three of us approached her and one guy said, "List with me, I'm a RE/MAX realtor." The other guy said, "List with me, I'm a RE/MAX realtor." I said I wrote the book on real estate, and I got the listing agreement. I made $40,000 and they made nothing. They knew everything and made nothing. I knew nothing and made everything, because I wrote a book.

# The 2020 Recession is Your Biggest Investment Opportunity

## Robert Rolih

**Robert Rolih:**

Hi, hi Raymond.

**Raymond Aaron:**

Hi. This is Raymond Aaron, New York Times top 10 bestselling author and professional speaker for 37 years, but I'm not going to do any speaking here. I'm just introducing a dear friend from Slovenia in the middle of Europe. A lot of people have never heard of Slovenia, but I have grown to love it. It's possibly the most beautiful country I've ever, ever seen. No litter. Everybody loves each other. It's the only country in the world that has love in its name, a huge distinction and they deserve it. But what this talk is about is not love. It's money. And I have on the line, Robert Rolih. It's an unusual spelling. R-O-L-I-H. R-O-L-I-H

**Raymond Aaron:**

If you wish to look him up. He's all over the internet. He's one of the wisest men in the world in terms of investing correctly. There's a lot of garbage out there, but there's very little that's really, really good about investing. And Robert knows about it. He wrote the Million Dollar Decision to help, not big corporations, but the average person invest really, really wisely. And the reason that I brought him to you, my dear client right now is because this isn't a bad time as far as investment is concerned. Weirdly, this is a good time. Robert, do you want to talk about that?

**Robert Rolih:**

Yeah, let me just turn on my camera. So can you see me now?

**Raymond Aaron:**

I can.

**Robert Rolih:**

Okay, perfect. So there is an old saying in the investing world that says buy when there is blood on the streets, even the blood is your own. So the best time for investing is when everybody's panicking and when everybody is selling of course. But it's very hard to buy in this time in the hard times because we humans, we have this herd mentality and we try to follow the herd, but that is exactly what we shouldn't do when it comes to investing. So I think that this is an amazing opportunity for smart, longterm investors.

**Raymond Aaron:**

Well, I understand that when the trend is up, that's a good time to buy that you should follow the trend. So am I wrong and can you explain that?

**Robert Rolih:**

Yeah. So there are a lot of rules, when it comes to investing and some are meant to be broken, some are not meant to be broken. But if we take a look at the stock market historically,

historically the stock market has a big, big, big, big uptrend with ups and downs, and when these downs come it's very important to be prepared. Okay? Because I will later in my presentation, I will talk about why the stock market produced the best possible returns in the past and what will probably happen in the future. So when you follow the trend and when the long term trend for the stock market is up of course. And I will explain why later, you always need to buy the dip, if you are buying when there is a dip you can get the best possible returns and that is why smart investors are utilizing or maybe let's say buying when there are big, big, big panics and when people are starting to sell everything and so on.

**Raymond Aaron:**

I remember Warren Buffet announced a while ago when everybody loved the stock market and the stocks were sailing. They were so high. He said he had a billion dollars in cash. The [inaudible 00:04:05] why aren't you investing it? You're the smartest investor in the world. And he said, "I'm keeping it for when it's lousy and when it's lousy, I'm going to have a billion dollars of stocks that are on sale." Anyways, I don't want to talk to you anymore. I want you to talk to my clients. We've had enough chit chat. I want you to teach and teach and teach. And at the end I want you to take some of the questions that people have been putting in the question's area and answer. So if at any time [inaudible 00:04:35] questions, just put them in the questions area and Robert go.

**Robert Rolih:**

Yeah, so I will answer all the questions at the end. Okay? And now I just want to check if you can see my screen so that there should be a photo of me on the screen. [crosstalk 00:04:55].

**Raymond Aaron:**

I see the big photo. I'm waiting for-

**Robert Rolih:**

Yes? Okay, perfect. So what would be the topics for today? Today the first topic will be a short intro to my investing system because when it comes to investing, you shouldn't just follow your emotions because you will make only bad financial decisions. So you need to have a system in place. And I will give you a very short introduction to my five step investing system that works like magic. Then the second topic will be the current situation on the markets. What is happening, what will the 2020 bring into our world and so on. So what is happening on the market with different asset categories like gold, stocks, bonds and stuff like this. Then can this be a big investment opportunity for us? So this would be one of the most important topics of course for today. And I will share you my opinion, what is going to happen or maybe the scenarios that may happen until the end of this year and in 2021.

**Robert Rolih:**

And my favorite topic at the end, what are the best possible investment products in times like this or also in the good times and which products to avoid at all costs? Because the problem is with the financial industry, financial advisors, are usually pushing, selling the worst possible financial products and that is why people get very, very low returns or mediocre returns from their investments. So this is my favorite topic and I will also show you how did I learn all this stuff. So it will probably surprise you that 10 years ago I had no clue about personal finance. I had no clue about investing. So how come that I teach people all around the world now about these topics?

Well, it's an interesting story. I was born in a very, very small village with approximately 100 people living there. It was a big water village, a very poor village in a small country of only two million population.

**Robert Rolih:**

And when I was young, my parents were working in a socialistic factory and they had these minimum wages. We never had any money at home, so I can still remember my father, Jimi Hendrix hairstyle. Whenever I ask him for something, the reply was always the same, "Robert, we don't have any money, [inaudible 00:07:34]" And that was the story of my childhood. But I hit something in me that changed my fate. And that was that I loved to read books. So I would go to library in a city nearby and I would borrow these business books. Books about achieving something in life, books about goals, I think achieving and so on. And my favorite author at that time was the legendary Brian Tracy. You probably know him now. If you don't know him, here is a photo of him.

**Robert Rolih:**

Oops, sorry. Wrong photo, wrong photo. This is the right photo. So Brian Tracy, he's the bestselling author, a famous speaker and so on. So the book at the top right, Maximum Achievement was my favorite book at the time. So as luck would have it when I was studying and I was living in a student dorm, I got an idea and I started my own business. So this was in 2001 and after four years of hard work and sleepless nights, my business finally started to make a lot of profits and my business, my company organized an event, a seminar with the legend himself with Brian Tracy. So this was March 10th, 2005 we organized a big event with Brian Tracy as a speaker. So it was like dreams coming true for me and I made a lot of money that year, this was the first year that I made six figure income and it was like, "Wow, amazing."

**Robert Rolih:**

But you know what? Saving a lot of money brings all sorts of problems. And the biggest problem I had was, where to put it. And I'm not kidding, I was an entrepreneur and I didn't have a clue about personal finance and investing. So I trusted who? What do you think? Yeah, financial advisors, bankers, managers, and so on. So year after year, I gave them all of my business profits. And then after several years of doing that, me and my wife Sarah, we had a conversation about personal finance and she said, "Robert, maybe it would be a wise idea to just check what is going on, check out what is going on with all our investments." And I said, "Okay." So I ordered all the account statements and when they arrived, you know these envelopes? When they arrived and I opened them. Just like, "What? Are there some zeroes missing? "

**Robert Rolih:**

Money we worked hard to earn was mostly gone. I was totally devastated. And that was the start of the darkest period of my life. I started to lose the motivation to work in my company. I got depressed, we started to have fights with my wife and so on. So it was a really, really bad situation. But luckily, I had already signed an agreement with Brian Tracy for his fourth seminar with my company. And after the seminar I invited him, to dinner and I said to him, "Brian, I have some big problems, financial problems, and I would like, if you can help me a bit with them." So it's first 20 minutes of dinner, we were like I was talking and he was listening and I spilled all my problems. And then he said something. So Brian Tracy looked me straight in the eyes and he said something that totally changed my life.

**Robert Rolih:**

And it may as well change your life too. Robert it doesn't matter how much you earn, all that matters is if you have the skills to manage your money and to invest it. And at that moment I realized I don't have the skills. I blindly trust the financial industry. So I made perhaps the most important decision of my life. I will become one of the most financially literate people in this world no matter what. So in the next approximately seven years, I invested heavily in my financial education. I read more than 300 books. I attended all of the best seminars about investing and money management around the world. So I was building my financial [inaudible 00:12:09], I was building my financial [inaudible 00:12:12] and this is the photo of me then. No Photoshop. So after the seven years of hard work, you might say, "Robert can not go wrong anymore. He knows it all."

**Robert Rolih:**

But you would be mistaken. Why? Because only after these seven years I started to learn that there are some small details, tiny details in the investment world. And if you don't know them, the financial industry will crush you. And I had to learn about these details on my own. Nobody, I told those seminars, nobody in all those books talked about these details and I learned them on my own. And now I have an important question for you. Would you like to learn what these details are today? Yes or no? I'm not going to share them with you. Okay, Okay. I will. I will. So today I will share these details with you with the help of the investing system that I first developed for myself. And then I started to share this system with clients all around the world. The name of the system is the Millionaire Money Making Machine investing system, and in the last years, I was really, really lucky and honored to be able to share this system with hundreds of thousands of people all around the world.

**Robert Rolih:**

This is the photo from my biggest seminar to date more than 2000 people in the audience. This is one of my London events where I shared the stage with Gary Vaynerchuk. This is one of my Moscow events. I am very popular also in Russia, a very interesting country and I am the number one public speaker or number one expert when it comes to investing in Russia right now. So I have seminars from the Netherlands, Sweden, UK. I have online events for U.S., for Canada, for Australia, for all the countries. And of course, I also published my book, The Million Dollar Decision that quickly became a number one international bestseller and the book was also translated into Chinese Mandarin. It was published in Taiwan, it was published in Bulgaria, it was published in India and so on. So yeah, and all of this brought me, of course a lot of media attention.

**Robert Rolih:**

I was featured in more than 50 newspapers, TV stations, online media and so on [inaudible 00:14:47], Business Insider, Newsmax TV, Russian TV, European TV stations and so on. So if I just sum it up, knowing the right details gets you a great return, ignore them and you just crash and burn. So when it comes to investing, you need to know the right details. Now how can you learn the right details and how can you win the financial game of life? The best way, I think is to learn and follow my system. So let me give you a very short overview of this system. If you want to win the financial game of life, you need to take five steps. Okay? Just five steps. The first step is the most important one. These are the foundations. You need to learn some important personal finance concepts.

**Robert Rolih:**

You need to understand how money works. You need to be able to manage your money properly. I call this increase your financial wisdom. So this is the first step, the most important one. Without this step, nothing will work. The second step is for people who understand that there are certain things that we cannot predict in life. This is to protect yourself, so protect yourself. So before you go on and try to get great returns with your money, you first need to protect yourself. And in my system, we use two tools to protect ourselves. The first door is insurance policies and the second tool are precious metals, gold and silver. Then the fourth step, if you have my workbook ready and printed, write down, grow your golden goose. So write down, grow your golden goose. These are your long term investments. These investments are the key to success in life, the financial success in life, and you need to have them in order to build your opinion book in order to increase your financial security power and maybe for schooling of your children and stuff like this.

**Robert Rolih:**

So grow your golden goose, these are your long term investments and long term investing in my system is 10 years plus. So you invest in a certain asset category or a financial product for at least 10 year periods. Okay? You don't sell after four years. You don't sell after five years, but you keep that money for a long time period. Okay? At least 10 years. Then the next step is for people who are impatient like me. It accelerates your returns. There are some strategies, more short term strategies where you can achieve better returns compared to your long term investments. But of course, this comes at an additional risk. So higher possible returns, but of course also a high risk. And the last part of my system is the answer to the question, why? Why am I doing all that? It's because you have certain dreams, certain goals, you want to achieve something in your life, you want to achieve a certain lifestyle and so on.

**Robert Rolih:**

So this is the system and it looks very simple and easy. But unfortunately, the financial industry put a lot of big hurdles on the way. The first big hurdle is that financial literacy is just not available for most people. And in our school systems, they don't teach us about personal finance and investing. Do you agree? So we all grew up without financial knowledge. Okay? I grew up totally financially illiterate. The game of law and the game of protecting ourselves and long term investing, these two games are rigged. This means that they are set up in such a way that only the financial industry is winning. And we are always losing. My case in point, the most popular financial products and the most popular life insurance products are basically the worst possible financial products out there. Why? Because of the fees.

**Robert Rolih:**

And in the second part of my webinar, I will show you how this works and how small fees can eat up most of your future returns. And in many cases, even the money you have invested. So these two games are really, really, really very hard to win. And today I will show you how to win them. The game of short term investing, it's the same story or maybe even worse because 19 out of 20 investors, short term investors lose their money and on average discrepancy in just four months. So with all these games being rigged, how the hell can we achieve our big dreams and even share our wealth? There's no way, but is there a solution for all this mess? And my answer is a resounding yes.

With free areas of financial wisdom, you will become one of the most financially illiterate people in the world and you will never need financial advisors anymore.

**Robert Rolih:**

With armor formula, I will give you a simple formula on how to choose the best possible insurance products and how to invest in gold and silver for the right reasons because most people invest in gold for totally the wrong reasons and I will also share with you with this formula all the other details that you need to understand before you invest in precious metals, we will feed our golden goose with the grain system. This system will help you accumulate two to five times more money compared to investing in the standard financial products that the financial industry recommends so much, much, much, better returns much, much, much smarter products compared to what your financial advisor recommends. We'd start the income builder. I will show you how you can win the short term trading game without trading. So no trading, totally passive strategy and it's quite unusual.

**Robert Rolih:**

But later I will maybe just take five minutes to explain this to you. And the last thing to know with all these systems in place. You will be able to reach your goals fast. So this is the entire system that I created for myself and then for my clients. And today of course I will not have enough time to go through the entire system. Usually, it takes me two full days to cover the entire system, at my live seminars and so on. But today I would like to give you, let's say two key messages or maybe one keys a part of my system. This is the long term investing that is the most important for you. Okay? So today you will learn some amazing things, some amazing strategies, some amazing information about long term investing that should be our most important investment strategy.

**Robert Rolih:**

And this is also the strategy that will help you to make it big during this recession. Okay? So I will give you really the most important part of my system today. And at the end of this webinar, I will also, invite you to join my online course that covers all of the details, all of the systems, all of the subsystems. Okay? And that will give you a very special offer that we agreed on with Raymond before this webinar. So it will be a really, really special offer if you want to learn all of the details and the entire system. So today, a lot of great value, you will be amazed, but if you want to learn the entire system, you will have an option to do that at the end of this webinar. Now, before we go into the content, some illegal stuff, I'm not financial advisor, okay?

**Robert Rolih:**

Everything that I share today is just my opinion and nothing constitutes financial or other professional advice. And if I mentioned any stocks or funds and so on, this is just for illustration. Okay? So this is something that you need to understand now, 4th of March. First let's move to the first topic and this is COVID-19 recession. What is happening? What could happen in the future and could this be a big opportunity for all of us? So 4th of March, I should have been in Moscow delivering my live seminar there. But of course, with my promoter, we agreed that I will not travel there because I saw what is going on with the Coronavirus and even though it was possible to get there, but I said no way because they can basically stop the flights when I'm there or something.

**Robert Rolih:**

So I'm very careful about these things and I decided to have this event online via live stream. So online stream and when I finished this seminar, it was like the end of the world. When I checked my email, when I checked the news, it was like . . . My promoter from the Netherlands, who also works with Tony Robbins said, "Robert, everything has been canceled, everything has been postponed, all the events, everything." Then I checked some news sites, cities were being locked down, the whole countries were being locked down. It was like, "Wow, what's happening?" So I think that this was the first day where the world realized that this is a very serious thing. The COVID-19 is a really serious thing that can have a huge effect on our lives and on our market, stock markets and all the other markets around the world. And also celebrities were getting infected and so on.

**Robert Rolih:**

And the stock market, this is my screenshot that I took at that time. It was like 40% down. Dow Jones went down 40% in just a couple of weeks. It's unprecedented. It was like the first time in history that something like this happened. Even gold a safe haven usually, went down with the stocks and maybe I will later to explain why. So it was like, what's happening? So what this might take on the COVID-19 recession in the making? On the 1st of March, before Warren Buffet, before [inaudible 00:26:19], before all these big investment gurus realized that something really terrible is happening. I wrote in very interesting article on my blog titled COVID-19 a global crisis in the making. And I talked about that COVID-19 was not the only reason why the stock is tanking there is another reason or there was another reason and that is the stock market was overvalued, overheated for a long time.

**Robert Rolih:**

And I started to prepare my clients for the next recession already in the last months of the year, 2010 '19 so last year on the 14th of November, I sent all of my clients a video with the recession warning. And I talked about that the federal reserve. United States federal reserve is basically force-feeding the economy with credit and this [inaudible 00:27:27] bubble will need to pop sooner or later. And then in January I have regular updates for my clients, for my course clients and I showed them how to prepare themselves for the recession and what should they do because of what will happen. But this was before the Coronavirus. I didn't know at the time that the Coronavirus will have such a huge effect, but the stocks were overvalued. This is the Warren Buffett indicator.

**Robert Rolih:**

It shows you the ratio between the value of the entire United States stock market versus gross domestic product. And as you can see here, this number means overvalued. So if it's more than 140 it's really, really highly over budget. It was like 160 before the dot com crash. It was like 117 before the financial crisis and now we close almost 150 so then the U.S. unemployment was at historic lows and when the employment is at historic lows, the next move is always it goes up, so there is some kind of recession because of the crazy cycles because of the market cycles and so on. So this is the contrarian indicator. Now I was preparing my clients for several months and now the question for you is, could these be a big opportunity for you? Okay? Now one of my favorite quotes says, "Recession is just a transfer of wealth from people who are not prepared and don't know the right details to people who are prepared and know the right details."

**Robert Rolih:**

So this is one of my favorite quotes. So recession is just a transfer of wealth. Okay? Now if you want to understand what is going on around the world right now, you need to understand two concepts. You need to understand the concept of acute versus chronic pain, okay? Or problem. So what is the acute problem? Acute problem is condition that is severe and sudden. Okay? Like a broken bone. Okay? If you break a bone, you fall from a tree, you break a bone. It's a big problem. But you need to go to a doctor and they give you [inaudible 00:30:04] and they fix you up and then a couple of months you are again healthy and you can run around. Okay? So this is an example of acute problem. So it's a short term problem. Okay? And we can find the solution for this problem.

**Robert Rolih:**

And then there are chronic conditions or chronic problems. Now, chronic conditions, by contrast, they persist for a long period of time, like Asthma or Arthritis when we don't know how to cure them. In this situation, with COVID-19 most people think that this is a chronic condition, that it's a total panic, that you need to sell everything that the world will never be good again and so on. But I think, I strongly believe that this is not correct and that the problems we are facing now are acute. Okay? And that they have a solution. Now, for now, we don't have a solution yet and we don't know how much time it will take to find a solution a medical solution.

**Robert Rolih:**

Maybe a cure or [inaudible 00:31:19], or something like this. So we don't know if this will take three months or six months or one year or 18 months or two years. We don't know that.

Maybe their will be some kind of magical solution in one month. You never know. Anything can happen, but we will find a way to solve this problem. We will find solutions because humankind always finds solutions and this is something, we need to understand that we will find solutions and people who can keep their heads cool right now and who think long term can have a huge advantage and can turn this recession into a big opportunity.

## PART 1 OF 4 ENDS [00:32:04]

**Robert Rolih:**

And can turn this recession into a big opportunity. Okay? Let me show this with a very, very interesting, story that I heard from a person that you might know and for him, Raymond Aaron. We had a Skype call with Raymond two weeks ago and he told me a story about a big tire graveyard in Canada. I think that it's somewhere near Toronto. There is a small town and near this town there was this big, big, big tire graveyard. I don't remember the name of the town. Sorry?

**Raymond Aaron:**

Hagersville Ontario.

**Robert Rolih:**

Okay, perfect. Perfect.

**Raymond Aaron:**

And it was a dump site for rubber tires.

**Robert Rolih:**

Yeah. So Raymond told me this story and it's really a story that hits home. And you need to understand this story if you want to understand this crisis. When Raymond was starting his career, he was into real estate and he was buying and selling real estate. So one day there was a big fire at this tire graveyard. So a big fire started to burn. And do you know how burning rubber smells? Now multiply that by a million. And you will get what happened there. So all the people were fleeing the city. It was like a catastrophe and everybody wanted to get rid of the real estate there. So Raymond went to the city and he met with the realtor there and he said, "I want to buy some pieces of real estate." And the realtor said, "Are you crazy? Everybody's fleeing the city and you want to buy real estate here. Are you crazy?" But Raymond did and he got a lot of great deals, dirt cheap deals. And he bought some pieces of real estate there.

**Robert Rolih:**

Now what happened after that? In the next month, the fire was gone, the city was cleaned and the life returned back to normal. And Raymond was able to sell this real estate for a much, much, much higher price. And this story can really give you a good idea of what is happening right now. So when everybody's panicking and everybody's thinking that this is a chronic problem, because also in this city, all of the people thought that it's over, that the town is over and that the life will never be the same again or they will never be able to live again in this town. But in reality, the problem was acute. Okay. And the same thing goes on in the world today. So this is something that you need to really, really, really understand.

**Robert Rolih:**

Okay. Now how to get the best possible returns by understanding these principles. The best way to do it is just to follow my system, especially the part where I talk about long term investing. So grow your golden goose and my G.R.A.I.N. System. Now we all know that we should invest for the long run. For pension, for security, for financial power, to just get great returns, for our children and so on. But there is a big problem when it comes to long term investing. And that is that the game of investing is rigged. And these guys, the financial advisors, will try to sell you the worst possible investment products. Why? Because they benefit the most from these products and then the companies they work for and so on. So let me show you how this works. And if you understand this, you will understand almost everything about investing. Okay? So pay attention. This part is really crucial for your investment needs in the future.

**Robert Rolih:**

If you want to understand the long term investing, you first need to understand the key investing principle. The key investing principle is compounding. Okay? Compound interest. Now, the boring, technical definition says you earn interest or return on your principal and on the accumulated interest of previous periods. So the balance doesn't merely grow, but it grows at an increasing rate. Now, this is theory, okay. But now let's take a look at practice.

**Robert Rolih:**

How does this work in practice? Let's say that you invest $10,000 and let's say that you have 10% annual growth. So 10% was historic annual growth for stocks. So average annual growth for stocks, historic growth, was 10% annually. Now if you have 10,000 and if this grows by 10% after the first year you will have, you probably guessed it right, 11,000. But the next year it will not be 12,000, it will be a bit more because also the interest from the previous period was getting compounded, was growing. So it's 12,100 now and it goes on and on and on. So these numbers start to grow exponentially. And after 40 years, you already have $452,000. All from a $10,000 investment. So that's times 45, okay? So this is the power of compounding.

**Robert Rolih:**

And because compounding is such a powerful principle, Albert Einstein said, "Compound interest is the eighth wonder of the world. He who understands it, earns it. He who doesn't, pays it." So let me show you how people who don't understand this principle pay a lot of money because of their ignorance. So let's say that you grow zero. You don't invest. After five years, you still have zero. After 20 years, you still have zero and you won't believe it, but after fourth years, you still have zero. So if you don't invest, if you don't utilize this most powerful investing principle, you will not earn any money when investing, because you will not be investing. You will not be utilizing this most powerful investing principle.

**Robert Rolih:**

So let me give you another example. Let's say that you save $5 per day. And I believe that anybody can save. If you have a normal paycheck, or if you are a small business owner or whatever, this is like nothing for you. So if you invest just $5 per day, this is $1,825 per year. And if you do that over 40 years, you have invested 73,000 of your money. Okay? $73,000 of your money. But because of the compounding principle and because of the market growth, and I used 9% annual growth here, okay, so I didn't go with 10% like it was historic growth for stocks. I went with nine. You got amazingly $657,000 just in returns.

**Robert Rolih:**

So your pension pot is $730,000. So this means, that if you are not investing, you are basically leaving all that money on the table. So $657,000 on the table, and this is the cost of not investing for the long run. In other words, small investments can make you wealthy if you start now. There is a Japanese proverb that says, when is the best time to grow a tree? And the answer is, 10 years ago. But if you haven't done that 10 years ago, the next best time is right now. So you should invest, you should start invest right now. And of course, 2020 will probably be one of the biggest investment opportunities in our lifetime. Simple as that because the market went down in a such a aggressive move, and probably it will go down even further. Okay. It will go down even further because in the next year, as you can see, the economy is at a standstill, and companies are firing people. So it will be a very, very big recession. But like I said, we will get over it. We will survive this recession and we will be stronger after this recession. And people who started to invest during 2020 will probably be the biggest winners of this period.

**Robert Rolih:**

So how to invest properly? What kind of financial products to you use? Which asset categories to use for investing? Let's take a look at the G.R.A.I.N. System. The first letter in the system is grow the right assets. Because if you don't grow the right assets, it's game over from the start. Okay? So the big question is what to invest in? What are the best financial products? So let's take a look. What are the options? So what are the options for long term passive investments? Okay, and here I'm talking only about passive investments. I'm not talking about active investments like investing in your own business or investing in real estate because these two types of investments are active investments, where you need to work hard to make some money out of them?

**Robert Rolih:**

Okay. So now we are talking about money working for you, basically. So what are the options? The first option are stocks. You are basically investing in companies. When you buy a stock, you become a co-owner of a certain company. Then bonds. Bonds, like government bonds. So just two things about bonds. If you don't know what this product is, just keep in mind that first, it's very safe. So you're just lending some money to the government. And the government then gives you some interest because they borrowed your money.

**Robert Rolih:**

So it's very secure but very low returns. Okay? So bonds are very secure but they give you very low returns, maybe in a region of two, 3% per year. Then precious metals, gold, silver. Then you can keep your money. Sorry, bank deposits. So the next one is bank deposits. And the last one is keeping your money under the mattress. Okay, so these are the options. And now what are the best options? But in order to get to the best options, we first need to eliminate some really, really bad options. So which options are the worst? Let's take a look. The first is keeping your money under the mattress. Now this is okay. If you keep your money under the mattress, for maybe a short time period, for a couple of months, for maybe one year. And in this situation, it's not a bad idea to have some money in cash.

**Robert Rolih:**

And I have some money in cash because I'm waiting for the right opportunities now. So for short time periods, keeping your money under the mattress is a good idea. But when it comes to long time period, like four years, five years, 10 years, it's a big no, no. Why? Because of the inflation. Prices are going up all the time. And if you keep your money under the mattress for 10 years, your money will lose approximately one quarter of the purchasing power. Okay? So in other words, prices will go up by 25% in 10 years. So your money will be worth less and less. And in two decades, you will only have half of the purchasing power that you have today. So it's not smart to keep your money under the mattress.

**Robert Rolih:**

The second worst option, you've probably guessed it, it's bank deposits. Banks give you almost nothing in interest right now. So you are still losing money accounting for inflation. So when you account for inflation, you are still losing purchasing power. What about precious metals? Good or bad? Most people say, "Hey, great. Great option." But unfortunately, they are mistaken. Why? Because precious metals, historically, they produced worse returns than bonds. They just kept their volume with inflation, and just a bit more. So average annual returns for gold and silver were just around 2% annually. So would you be happy with 2% annually? Okay. So I'm not using gold when I want to get great returns. I'm just using gold in my system in the second part, protect yourself. Okay? So gold, we are just using it in the second part for financial protection. But we don't expect huge gains from gold. And this is something that a lot of people don't understand and it's very important.

**Robert Rolih:**

And now only stocks and bonds are left. And these were historically the most profitable options. Now which one produced better returns? You probably guessed it, stocks. Stocks are volatile, but also they produced much, much, much higher returns in the past. This is one of the most important charts when it comes to investing. This is the chart of real returns, after inflation returns, for different asset categories in the past. So this is from 1926 to 2016. Okay? Almost 100-year period. And this you can see here, only stocks, the blue line, produced huge returns and everything else was pretty average or miserable. Okay? So only stocks produced amazing returns in the past. And this is not like a bit better returns compared to bonds or gold.

**Raymond Aaron:**

Robert, we can't see the graph.

**Robert Rolih:**

You cannot see what?

**Raymond Aaron:**

We can't see the graph. We just see, there it is. Thank you.

**Robert Rolih:**

Yeah. Okay? Now do you see it? Yeah, okay. So the important thing is that this difference is not small. It's huge difference. It's like 40 or 50 times better returns compared to everything else. Okay? So why were stocks historically such a good option? And the reason is because stocks are companies. When you invest in stocks, you are investing in the most dynamic part of our world. You are investing in companies that are innovating all the time, that are producing new value, bringing new value to the market, they're adapting to market conditions and so on. That is why companies produced the best possible returns in the past.

**Robert Rolih:**

Now, will it be the same in the future? And my answer it you never know. Nothing is 100%, okay? You need to be very careful when it comes to investing because nothing is 100% sure. So if the world will survive, if the aliens don't invade, if there is no global catastrophe and we all die, then companies will continue to produce the best possible returns. Okay. So it's like 99% chance or probability that the same will happen in the future. But of course, there is always 1% probability that may be something really strange will happen and we will all die in the big laser blast from the alien spaceship or something. So we need to understand these probabilities. So stocks were the best option in the past and 99% probability is that there will be the best possible option also in the future. Okay? Because they are growing, they are adapting themselves and they are bringing new value and so on.

**Robert Rolih:**

So, most of our long term portfolio will probably be in stocks. Okay. It depends on your age of course. Because if you are 70 years old, it will be a bit different, okay, because you will need to have a lot of money in bonds also. But if you are younger, then you will probably have the biggest part of your portfolio in stocks. I have most of my money in stocks and now in cash because I'm waiting for the right opportunities.

**Robert Rolih:**

Now let's pick some stocks. Let's pick Apple, let's pick Amazon, let's pick Tesla, let's pick Nike, Disney and so on. Is this a good choice? And the answer is no. Even though these companies are great, it's not a wise choice. Why? The reason these because any company can go down or out of business. Let me give you a famous example. Do you remember a company called Nokia? 12 years ago, Nokia was the leader in the mobile phones. But today they are nowhere. Their stock fell by 97%. So 12 years ago, Nokia was just like Apple today, but now it's almost gone. So that is why it's very risky to invest in individual stocks, and you should never do it. I don't invest in individual stocks. I never invest in individual stocks and I never will. It's like gambling with your money.

**Robert Rolih:**

But, of course, when you invest in the whole stock market, then it's another thing, and I will explain this in a minute. So the second reason why we don't invest in individual stocks is that nobody can pick just the right stocks. Stock market analysts and gurus are famous for their predictions that are wrong. David Dreman did a big study of stock expert predictions and he found out that they were historically wrong in 77% of cases. So it will be much better if you listen to them and just do the opposite. Okay? So that is why we never invest in individual stocks. But like I said, if you invest in a big basket of stocks, then you can be pretty, pretty sure, it's never 100%, but you can be pretty, pretty sure that these stocks will grow over time because you are not investing in individual stocks but in a whole stock market. And because the financial industry found out that people are afraid of investing in individual stocks, they proposed a solution. Decades ago they proposed a solution.

And the solution was mutual fund. So when investing in mutual funds, and this is the most popular investing product all around the world, also in Canada.

**Robert Rolih:**

So if you invest in mutual fund, you are basically investing in a big basket of stocks. And that's a great idea. That's a great idea because you are lowering the risk, you are lowering the risk. You're not investing in individual stocks. But why did I tell you that investing in mutual funds is one of the worst ideas that you can get and that this will destroy your financial future? And the reason is because of the small details. The devil is always in the details.

**Robert Rolih:**

So let me show you the most important thing that you need to understand about all longterm investments. Okay? And if you are investing, like most people do, in mutual funds or in whole life insurance, this is the type of life insurance where you invest something and you are also insured for life. So it builds cash value. So these two products are the worst possible products, mutual funds and whole life insurance. And now I would show you why. So pay attention.

**Robert Rolih:**

When you invest in mutual fund or whole life insurance, first you pay a service fee or entry commission. Then you pay when you want to exit, let's say after 10 years, you want to exit this product, you pay exit fee. And these two fees are approximately zero to 3%, okay? Depends on the product, but zero to 3%. But I have some good news for you. And these good news are that these two fees are not important. Why? Because they are just one time fees. Okay? And they will not affect your long term returns by much. But there is another fee that can wreak havoc in your investment account. And this fee is management fee, or total expense ratio, or expense ratio. This fee is deducted from your account every single year. For as long as you are in this product, this fee is being deducted every single year. Okay? And on average, it's around two to 2.5% annually.

**Robert Rolih:**

And now you will say, "But Robert, that's not a lot. They take 2% and I keep 98. That's perfectly okay, right?" Wrong. Wrong. Why is that wrong? What did you forget to account for? We forgot to account for compounding principle. And I call this the dark side of compounding. Not only your returns are getting compounded when you invest, but also the commissions are getting compounded. So that is why I call this the dark side of compounding.

**Robert Rolih:**

Now let me show you the dark side of compounding, the effect of this, in the previous example. So if there were no fees, by investing $5 per day, you would just have the entire pension pot for yourself, 730,000. But, when you account for the 2% management fee, this will not amount to 730,000, but the biggest part of the pie will be eaten by the financial industry. So you will only be left with 350,000 and the majority of your money will be taken by the financial industry through small commissions and fees. So this is really something that nobody in the financial industry will ever tell you about. Why? Because it's not in their interest, because they make a lot of money when you don't know these things. Okay? So small fees, small fees, can basically halve your long term returns. Small fees can halve your long term returns. Now, is this a good thing for the financial industry? It's perfect. But for us it's a really bad thing.

**Robert Rolih:**

So would you like to learn the solution? If your answer is yes, then here is the solution. Instead of investing in mutual funds, I used to invest in mutual funds when I was younger and I didn't know these details. But right now, I'm investing in a different product, much better product. It's called the index fund. Simplified, index fund is just a very similar product to a mutual fund, but with much lower commissions and fees. The expense ratio, or management fee, for mutual funds, it's two to 2.5% annually. But for index funds, is just 0.05 to 0.5% annually. So approximately 10 time lower commissions and fees. Okay? And this is key. So when investing in index funds, you keep the lion's share of all the returns.

**Robert Rolih:**

So let's take a look at the previous example. So here, when it comes to mutual funds, the financial industry would you take all that money through these small commissions and fees? But, when you invest in index funds, the in the financial industry will keep or take just a small portion of your money, and the lion's share will be yours. So that is why I love to invest in index funds.

**Robert Rolih:**

Let me give you a real life example. So this is comparison between two funds. The blue line is one of the most popular mutual funds. It's called Fidelity Magellan. Okay? It's one of the most popular mutual funds in the world. And the red line is one of the most common, or one of the average index funds. It's called SPY and it just follows the S&P 500 index, so the biggest United States companies. And why did I choose these two for comparison? Because they are both investing in the same basket of stocks. Okay? Because you cannot compare, for example, pharmaceutical mutual fund to a technology index fund. This is like comparing apples and oranges or bananas. So you need to compare something very similar, something that invests two products that invest in the same stocks. And here we are comparing two products that are investing in basically the same stocks. There is 95% stock overlap here.

**Robert Rolih:**

And as you can see, the ups and downs come at exactly the same times. But the difference is huge. So if you invested 10,000 in both products a couple of decades ago, now you would have 14,000 if you invested in mutual fund. But if you just chose a better investment vehicle, index fund, you would now have $61,000. A bit of a difference, huh? So this is the difference between mutual funds and index funds and the same goals with whole life insurance. But it's even worse for the whole life insurance. Okay. Because they have additional fees on top of the mutual fund fees there. And as you can see here, the difference between these two funds is growing larger and larger. Why? The first reason is because of the difference in fees. And the second reason is because of compounding principle, because the longer you keep this investment, the bigger the difference. Okay? And all the difference is basically the difference in commissions, compounded.

**Robert Rolih:**

That is why also Warren Buffett is a very big advocate of index funds, just like me. Okay. So today we learned about the first letter in the G.R.A.I.N. System, what to invest in. But of course, if you want to really invest the right way for the long run and if you want to really get the maximum profits, you need to understand couple of other things. You need to understand the other letters also. The most important thing is that there are more than 4,000 index funds available all around the world. And most of them are not a good choice for long term investors. A lot of them are short term trading vehicles. A lot of them have higher fees, they have similar fees to mutual funds. The financial industry is very cunning. They just name something index fund and you think you're buying index fund, but then you take a look at the commissions and they are very similar to mutual funds. So you need to really know what to choose. You need to know which index funds are the best. And that is why, because this is a very difficult task, I did something for my clients. And this is that I prepared my personal selection of 14 index funds that are the best of the best. They have the lowest possible fees.

## PART 2 OF 4 ENDS [01:04:04]

**Robert Rolih:**

This are the best of the best. They have the lowest possible fees. They are suitable for long term investors and they have the highest profit potential because there are certain industries that are already mature industries or they are already going down. So, we don't like to invest in this kind of industries and the same goals with different markets different regions. We don't invest in regions that have no potential.

**Robert Rolih:**

So, I made this important selection for you. I spent more than 100 hours analyzing different regions, different industries, different index funds and I created this list for you and all of the index funds that I personally invest in are on this list. So, you get the solution, you get the names, you get everything here and then you will not invest in all 14 of them. I only invest in six of them.

**Robert Rolih:**

So, you would maybe invest in one, two, three, four, five, six of them not in all 14. That is why I will give you my satellite strategy. So, these will help you to choose the ones that you will personally invest in and you'll see it's simple and easy and it's a bit different depending on your age and depending on your goals, but this strategy will give you the solution. Do we give you the ones that you will invest in and at the end I will also explain how to invest in index funds. I will explain which brokers to use in order to invest in index funds.

**Robert Rolih:**

So, which brokers have the best. I have a special selection also for Canadian market, for US market, for European market, for UK market and so on and when to invest and this is really an important thing when to invest, now in the next year there will be huge opportunities and I talked about yesterday, see you later. I update my clients about this.

**Robert Rolih:**

So when you invest in index funds, the best companies in the world are working for you in a basic way. So this is a basic investment vehicle and you can use it in order to get the best possible returns, especially in the times like this.

**Robert Rolih:**

Couple of testimonials, thank you for a well-informed course where not only was I able to fully understand the ins and outs of long term investing, but given a step by step guide on exactly how to implement what I have learnt. At the end the only decision that was left was to ask myself when I would take action. So this is one of my UK clients.

**Robert Rolih:**

This is one of my US clients. I thought I knew almost all there is to know about investing. But I put my emotions aside and I learned from Robert's expertise. When Robert showed me the true cost of fees and over a long time period. I was stunned. I took immediate action to bring by investments in line with Robert's recommendations. Ralph trust that his financial advisor before he bought my course and when he went through my course, he fired the financial advisor and he learned that his financial advisor put on top of the fees that he was paying in mutual funds, she put another percent of his own fees. So it was like crazy. So, he basically saved more than $100,000 just by switching from his financial advisor to my selection of index funds. Now to wrap everything up, I would like to give you my seven keys or seven steps for successful investing in the turbulent times like this.

**Robert Rolih:**

The first thing is, the first key is become financially literate. You need to understand how money works. You need to understand the market cycles. You need to understand what is happening in the financial world out there and the first part of my system will be focused on that. So increase your financial wisdom. We'll teach you how to manage your money, how to understand all the things that are going on around us and so on and this will be very simplified. I always explain things in simplified way so it will not be like a lot of technical terms and so on, but I explain things simply then protect yourself before you invest for gains. So first comes the financial protection.

**Robert Rolih:**

The second gear protects yourself and only after that comes the returns then don't buy what the financial industry commands. If your banker, if your financial advisor, if your fund manager or whatever, if they offer you something, the good thing to do is to say no thank you because they will always offer the worst possible products, the products where they profit the most.

**Robert Rolih:**

Then lower the commissions and fees. If you lower the commissions and fees that you are paying, you will get maximum returns and one of my strong points is that I'm not affiliated with any brokers. I'm not affiliated with any advisors and so on. I give you the right knowledge and then you go and you open your own brokerage account. I am not the affiliated, I don't care where you do open it. I have some recommendations for different markets but I don't get anything. So, I don't earn money based on what you invest in I earned money only for my knowledge, only for my courses.

**Robert Rolih:**

So, take advantage of market panics. This is something that we will have an opportunity to do in the next year or so, Think long term. When you do the opposite with what the court does, you will always profit the most. So think long term and understand that this crisis will sooner or later be over and the good times will return. Maybe the times will be different. Maybe the word would change, but we will have good times again and the last thing, one of my most popular quotes, this one was featured in a Yahoo final selection of 20 best quotes about investing. And I was on the number one on the list before Warren Buffett before elderly Watson. "Investing is simple, it's the financial industry that works hard to make it complex." Investing is simple. If you know what you are doing now you have three options how to proceed.

**Robert Rolih:**

The first option is to trust these guys and you know what will happen through your money. Then the second option is to become an active investor, active trader and these guys are constantly checking where are their stocks, what is happening to their portfolio, they are trading all the time, they are nervous. This affects their health, this affects their family and so on and they look like this and the third option, is to become a passive investor using my system and you will look like this, you will not be sun bathing all the time, especially not in the crown of Iris word.

**Robert Rolih:**

I mean when you learn my strategies, when you apply them in your life, your money will work hard for you basically. All my strategies that I teach are totally passive. No active trading, no staring at computer screen and clicking buy seven so on. So this is smart, long term investing for people who want to have time freedom for people who want to have hobbies for people who would like to spend a lot of time with their family, who want to focus on their work, on their business and so on. So you will not be wasting your time on investing, but you will know that you have a system in place that works hard for you and your money will be working hard.

**Robert Rolih:**

So the course fee, how much is the millionaire money making machine course? So this is, of course, I'm talking about the online course right now. Usually I have live courses in person, in different hotel rooms and so on. But right now, I'm only selling of course, my online courses. So the courses, $2,997 and what does it include? The first thing, three areas of Financial Wisdom. So everything about financial literacy and you will never need financial advisors when you go through the first thought.

**Robert Rolih:**

Then A.R.M.O.R Formula. So this is financial security for you and for your family. Insurance products, so everything about insurance products, we try some of the good ones, we try also the bad ones, [inaudible 01:13:54] to be careful about and so on. So everything about insurance and then Gold and Silver, how much Gold and Silver, how do you buy it and all the other details.

**Robert Rolih:**

Then longterm investing so we will gain with the grain money working caught for you my selection of index funds, we also cover Bonds and we also cover all the other details that you need to understand when it comes to longterm investing and get there fast.

**Robert Rolih:**

So how to achieve your financial goals. I started from scratch. I had no special talents, I had no money, my family was poor but I was able to achieve amazing things in my life and I will teach you in this part what strategies, what techniques did I use in order to make it big in my life and at the end, Asset Allocation, very important topic. How to allocate your money based on your age and based on your goals because, what do you invest in if you are 40 year old will differ from what you invest when you are 60 or 70 years old. So it's totally different for different ages. So, my promise for you is this will be the only passive investing course that you will ever need. Everything is included and I will lead you step by step.

**Robert Rolih:**

So money working card for you and all the strategies are basically a couple of testimonials. The first course that showed me in the most practical way what to do and how to do it, which buttons to click and how to get great returns when investing. This course gave me way more value than any other training to date. I quickly learned things that seemed like a science fiction to me just a week ago. Robert kept his promise and this is truly the only investing course that I will ever need. This is already famous tennis professional.

**Robert Rolih:**

Really honest advice, you can take action immediately. This will definitely take us as a family in a new direction and I just received that on Sunday. I had a webinar like this for the Netherlands one week ago or something and people are already using it, so Maciel I think it's pronounced on Sunday.

**Robert Rolih:**

So this Sunday I love it Robert. I'm getting so much new insights about how to set it up and by feel you really want to make it work without only making money. I lost 23,000 euros of course by an online binary scan two years ago and I wish I had known about this course and wasn't just trying to get rich fast. It took me one year to get over this and so on and so on.

**Robert Rolih:**

So I will also teach you how to avoid scams. I will also teach you a lot of other things that I didn't mention today, but everything is included.

**Robert Rolih:**

Now, you are a client of Raymond and the Raymond is my good friend and before this webinar we had the conversation and he said to me, "Robert, we really need to make an amazing offer for my list because the times are tough and the opportunities are big and I want as much people on my list to get this opportunity." So that is why I decided or we decided together with Raymond to give you a very special opportunity today.

**Robert Rolih:**

So, these opportunity, first I will give you a small discount and then I will also give you some additional gifts. So first, the discount, the small discount instead of $2,997 the fee for this course for you today will be nine nine seven dollars, so $997. Plus when you order today, you will get some additional gifts. Now this is the link when you order. So it's aaron.com/MoneyMakingMachine and Raymond, I don't know if it's possible to just post this link somewhere.

**Raymond Aaron:**

Well, Robert.

**Robert Rolih:**

If it's possible, maybe you can just post this link so they will be able to click on it or something. So it's aaron.com/MoneyMakingMachine and now about gifts. I prepared something really special for you today. The first gift, it's something that I usually don't including in this course because it's too valuable, and I said this separately, but today I will put this into the package. It's my Start Passive Income Builder. It's the fourth part of my system that I usually sell separately. This is an amazing artificial intelligence trading strategy for short term gains. So it's totally passive. It's not humans doing the trading, but its Artificial intelligence. It's not my system.

**Robert Rolih:**

A London team of traders and IP professionals create this system and in the last year it produced a little less than 60% annual return, six zero it's an amazing stuff.

**Robert Rolih:**

Money is in your investment account. You are not giving your money to them. Your money stays on your investment account and only the traits that the artificial intelligence is making are being copied to your account. It's an amazing system. Now, what is their offer? They are offering this system to people who pay 1,297 connection fee and then you'll split the profits with them 70 40. So, you keep 70% of the profits and they keep 40% of the profits.

**Robert Rolih:**

Now, because I personally, and this is all invite only stuff, you can not find this online. This is not something that they would offer to the public. This is invite only stuff. Now, the owner of the company, the trader who created the system, he's my good friend.

**Robert Rolih:**

I got to know him when I was trading and losing a lot of money, but we'd shortened trading in London that was approximately 12 14 years ago when I was young and stupid and I thought I can make money by trading Forex on my own. Of course, I lost almost the 100,000 euros doing that and then I stepped to the enough, but she's my good friend and what I did for my clients will blow you away.

**Robert Rolih:**

The agreement that I have with him for my clients, for my Mmm Course clients' is no connection, zero connection fee and there is only 80 20 profit split.

**Raymond Aaron:**

That's amazing.

**Robert Rolih:**

That's totally amazing because usually they just try to sell you some kind of subscription or connection fee and so on and then they run away with your money. But here money is in your account and they can not steal it only the traits are being copied. You can stop anytime you like. You can start anytime you like. You can stop using the system anytime you like you can withdraw anytime you like. It's your money, it's on your account, just the traits are being copied. And if they don't make you money, they don't get anything. They don't make a cent if they don't make a profit.

**Robert Rolih:**

So that is what I like and I really hate those financial advisors that are having this in place and the subscriptions and so on. So that is why I really, it took me a lot of time to convince him. But at the end I said to him this or nothing and he owned a couple of favors. So that is why we were able to do this deal. But this is an amazing stuff. So zero dollars connection fee and only profit split and that's it.

**Robert Rolih:**

And you get 80% of the returns and if they don't make profits, you pay zero. They don't make any money. So that is why we are all on the same side. There is no conflict of interest here and that is what I like here. So this, you will get this as a bonus if you order when you order today.

**Robert Rolih:**

Then the second bonus, I don't want to just give you a solution now and then nothing I want to be with you for the long run. So that is why I have for my Mmm clients, I have two times Q&A live online sessions, so two sessions per year. So if you have any questions, if you have any dilemmas, if you have any situations that you don't know how to solve them and so on, you can ask me that in those sessions.

**Robert Rolih:**

So usually annual subscription is 249 for this, but today I decided to give you this totally for free, but not only for one year, but for as long as I do this. Now, when I die, don't expect this any more from me. Okay?

**Raymond Aaron:**

Okay.

**Robert Rolih:**

So two sessions per year from now on to really be in touch with me all the time and to get the updates, to get the new information, to get questions to your answer, answers to your questions and so on. And bonus number three, something really special these time periods, the COVIT-19 recession I call this will be really interesting period. It's really hard period. We will need to be careful. We will need to work hard. We will need to adapt. But like I said, for smart investors, this will be one of the best opportunities in our lifetime.

**Robert Rolih:**

So I will give you my regular updates throughout the COVID-19 recession for as long as it will last. So these would be weekly updates. You will get this via email and you will be constantly in touch with me. So, I will tell you exactly when I'm buying what I'm buying from my list and so on. And that will give you the exact strategy that we'll be using throughout this period and weekly I will notify you when I'm doing something. So you will always know what to do when to do it and if you will have any questions, you will be able to ask me and I would answer.

**Robert Rolih:**

So, this will help you to turn this recession into big profits. This is totally free. I forgot to mention that. So you will get also this for free. So if I summarize, this special offer is only good for today. So, this is only good for today. You need to order today. You will be ordering through Raymond's company. So, you will be ordering through Raymond's company and you're just go to the link that that is published now. So aaron. com/MoneyMakingMachine without spaces. Money making machine.

**Robert Rolih:**

So, let me summarize. First you get the complete minimum money making machine home study course. This is an online course that you can go through from the leisure of your home and you will not be exposed to any viruses and so on and you will get a lifetime access to this. So, this is a lifetime access to this course and I also update it if something changes and so on.

**Robert Rolih:**

> Then you will get Star Passive Income Builder for free two times per year, Q&A live sessions with me online of course free and COVID-19 updates for free. So, all these for one time, payment of nine nine seven. So, this is not a subscription, this is not some kind of annual subscription. This is a one time payment of nine nine seven. So grab this opportunity, just go to this website and just the putting your details and click order and you will get X's details in 24 hours and then you will get all the updates and all the other bonuses you will get them via email. So, this is everything from my side Raymond, and now maybe we can go to question and answer.

**Raymond Aaron:**

> First of all, I want to comment.

**Robert Rolih:**

> Okay,

**Raymond Aaron:**

> I'm dazzled. I have been teaching wealth principles for 37 years, since May of 1983 and I was stuck to this computer. I was listening to every word. I was dazzled when you ask questions. I said, "Oh yeah, I know the answer." And then I would say it to myself and I was wrong. What? Now, the truth is, I've invested more in real estate than in stocks. But nevertheless, I thought I knew my stuff and I am dazzled. I'm so moved and I wish I could say something to you right now. I wish I could say I'm the first to join and the reason I can't is because lots of people have already joined lots of people. I can see this on my screen, you can't see it, but I can see it. I can screen see the numbers totaling up. So I'm in and my clients are in and I'm so happy

that you are going to be taking care of my clients and me. Your system is amazing and I love it.

**Robert Rolih:**

Yes it's amazing and then the best thing is that I don't come from the financial industry. I was a business owner and then I lost a lot of money and because of that I started to learn and this one of my strengths that I can explain things in simple terms and most financial experts, they can not do that because they have been in this industry for their whole life and I am some kind of outsider who came into this industry later, but I learned seven years every day I spent 10 hours per day learning this stuff and so that is why I can still understand how an everyday person feels about these things and that is why I give step by step solutions. I don't just tell you go and buy these index funds with a broker. I give you screenshots how to do it, step number one click here, step number two click here and so on. So it's really step by step system and you can do it even if you are not computer literate and stuff like this.

**Raymond Aaron:**

You're the only person in the financial industry who doesn't like high fees.

**Robert Rolih:**

Yeah, probably because the problem is that most financial advisors and gurus, they make money because they sell you financial products. They sell you some kind of financial product like their fund invest in my fund or whatever. But all these financial products that I am, let's say recommending to my clients, they are not mine. You will not be investing through my company. You will be investing through a regular broker like a Vanguard or Interactive Brokers and I'm not affiliated with these companies. You cannot be affiliated with them.

**Raymond Aaron:**

I've got to tell you one other thing that I really loved for your entire presentation. You were saying, "Here's how you make money in the long run." And I'm saying, "Hey, I'm 75 why aren't you talking about me? Why aren't you telling me anything? Why have you forgotten me? There's lots of my clients who are a little older in age. Why aren't you helping me?" And then right at the end you zinged us with 60% recurrence. Hello? Wow . . .

**Robert Rolih:**

[crosstalk 01:31:42] this would be a good option. Artificial intelligence trading would be a good option for you.

**Raymond Aaron:**

You're offering both high short term returns and high long term returns. What else is there?

**Robert Rolih:**

So, this is really an amazing solution and right now I'm swamped with orders, not here because I cannot see and how many people ordered. But in the last weeks we sold more than, so I got more than almost more than 500 clients for this course in just the last couple of weeks from all over door. Yesterday I got my first client from South Africa. I got for my first time for Mordovia, I got from Norway, from Australia, from Thailand or around the world. And they are just crazy about this, but it's worth it, it's totally worth it. So, we can maybe go to a question and answer session and I will answer questions that . . .

**Robert Rolih:**

I will be able to check them out. I'm not sure that I can see the questions. Oh yeah, I see them. But, I can only see one line at a time and it's almost impossible to check this out. Let me just try to . . .

**Raymond Aaron:**

I know when you click on it, you'll see below the full comment.

**Robert Rolih:**

Oh yeah, now I got it. I opened the full page now. Let me go through the questions. This was the start then. Where do we get index funds? So Yvonne, you buy index funds through a broker, through a stock broker and being my course, you will get a list of stock brokers from different countries and also for Canada because I have a lot of clients in Canada already and I did some research and I found the best brokers for you in Canada. So you will get this leads to when you go through my course and you will get the name of the company and then you just go to the website, click open an account and it just like opening a new bank account. You will need to verify yourself and then you will find your account and then you will be able to buy index funds and I have also screenshots help to go through these buying. It's very simple.

**Robert Rolih:**

Can you please repeat the course price? Our internet issues. So it's nine nine seven so after the discount, so it's nine nine seven. Yes, it's us dollars. Thanks Robert. I've already taken the offer. Perfect Carl. Thank you. No, this is us dollars. Again in dollars, he's 100% right about bank financial investments and mutual funds. We have lost so much, almost all of our life savings and it's still dropping because of COVID. The problem with mutual funds and the high fees that short bank is that even in good times you can lose a lot of money because these fees are so high that sometimes even if there are good times, they produce at the end of the year negative returns with this piece. So, it's really legalized crime something like this legalized stealing. I am 65 years, we will this be good for me in the short term. So Karen, if you would like to get some short term returns, I would say artificial intelligence.

**Robert Rolih:**

Also, get my asset allocation for people who are near retirement or retired. So you will have my asset allocation for 65 or older. And if you want to use something, maybe a smaller amount of money or a smaller percentage of your portfolio for artificial intelligence, this could be a very good option.

**Robert Rolih:**

How do you manage for those in Malaysia? Now, I don't know for Malaysia, I don't know the specifics of that market, but I have clients from all around the world and big brokers like Interactive Brokers and Vanguard. They are accepting clients from all around the world, basically from almost all the countries except for maybe South Korea or something.

**Robert Rolih:**

So I think that you will have no problem buying index funds through one of the brokers that is on my list. I never had any problems. And I have customers from Thailand to Singapore, Hong Kong, East Ireland, all the other countries. So it will not be a problem.

**Robert Rolih:**

Yeah. So if you have retirement plans, index funds can be a good decision to use in your retirement plan also, because when you invest in your retirement plan, you will need to choose which products will this money be invested in. And usually, this is automatic, but you can also change this. Okay? In your retirement account. You can also change this, and of course, if you choose index funds you will be much better off than with the regular mutual funds.

**Robert Rolih:**

Do we do the trading or do traders trade for us? And how much do you have to invest for the trading? So this is probably about artificial intelligence trading. So artificial intelligence trading, you will not be making any trades. Everything is automatic. You just connect to the system and from then on, so this is like 45 minutes. You need to open an account and connect to the system. And after that you don't need to do anything else. So it's totally automatic. You just see the returns on the chart.

**Robert Rolih:**

So everything is done by the artificial intelligence system that these are controlled by this team of traders, professional traders and they are doing everything for you so you don't need to do any trading, nothing. Totally passive.

**Robert Rolih:**

Frank, I see your question. In this circumstance, I would advise you to write an email to Raymond's team. So if you have this issue about money that you will get money in a week time, please send an email to Raymond's team. We will not be able to give you the same offer, because this offer is really only for today. But we will maybe give you a big different offer but of course this offer is just for today. So write an email to Raymond's team. [crosstalk 01:39:42]. Is there an email on the order form?

**Raymond Aaron:**

Let me give you an email address. Mpatel. M as in Mickey. Mpatel. M-P-A-T-E-L. Mpatel@aaron.com. That's A-A-R-O-N. Mpatel, like Michael. Mpatel@aaron.com. And you can ask him any questions if you have money coming in tomorrow, things like that or a payment plan or whatever your issue is. He's my chief financial officer. Mpatel@aaron.com. A-A-R-O-N.

**Robert Rolih:**

Star Passive Income Builder, produced 60% last year. What has it done in the five years prior to that? It didn't exist at the time. So this software or this artificial intelligence system has only been working for a little more than one year now. So it's totally a new system and it doesn't exist two years ago.

**Raymond Aaron:**

That's a good question.

**Robert Rolih:**

Yeah, that's a good question. Yeah. Mmm. Okay, totally blown away. Perfect. Thank you. Thank you, Manny. What have been historical returns from your index funds?

**Robert Rolih:**

So, when you invest in index funds, you, in the long run, the average annual returns are around 10% annually. This means that you double your investment in approximately six to seven years. But then, of course, it depends on when you start. If you start now when the prices are lower, you will get really amazing returns from these investments. If you start at, like three months ago, you wouldn't be buying it at the top. And I was, I showed you, I showed my clients, I was warning them that a [inaudible 00:05:56] the last six months. It was not a good idea to start investing in stock index funds. And I gave them and these alternatives worked like magic in these times, because my alternatives were put some of the money in bonds that were very good investment in the last period of time, and put some money in gold for a short time period, and keep some money in cash.

**Robert Rolih:**

So that was my recommendation. And Joe, when you buy this course, you will be able to watch my video seminars for my clients from January and March and so on. So you will be able to check this out.

**Robert Rolih:**

But yeah, you can expect for, let's say for the long run, approximately 10% or annually on every channel, but if you're starting in bad times like this, it can be more.

**Raymond Aaron:**

I'd like to add something to that, Robert.

**Robert Rolih:**

Yeah, go ahead.

**Raymond Aaron:**

The 10% is not because the fund manager is so clever. The 10% is because that's what the stock market is doing.

**Robert Rolih:**

That's right.

**Robert Rolih:**

Yeah. So when you invest in index funds, there is nobody choosing the stocks in this fund, and nobody's picking the stocks it's just investing in the whole market. Or in the whole, let's say pharmaceutical industry, and the whole technology industry in the whole Asian market, in the whole global economy, in the whole US market and so on and so on and so on.

**Robert Rolih:**

I've never done a course like this. If this isn't what I expected can I get my money back? All right, [Rachel Rochelle 00:07:33], I don't have money big guarantee for this course. But if you are not satisfied, I will gladly give you your money back. It's not a problem. I sometimes get a client who wants the money back and you, it's happened a couple of times in the past, but these were people like . . . There was a gentleman saying, "I thought that I would be using your strategies, but I'm already 80 years old" or something. And so, yeah. For some people maybe it's not the suitable course. But yeah, we can do that for you. No problem.

**Robert Rolih:**

Can you talk about toxic implications for Canadians buying non-Canadian index funds? No problem here. You will be buying that through Canadian broker and there will be no US withholding tax. So you will be just paying the capital gains tax. Just like if you buy stocks or mutual funds, it's totally the same. So when you invest in index funds, and this is just capital gains tax and that's it.

**Robert Rolih:**

What about ETFs? ETFs are the same thing as index funds. ETFs are the same thing as index funds. This is just another name for the same thing.

**Robert Rolih:**

Does start base of income statement connect your own brokerage account? Yes, Carl. So you will open your own brokerage account, you will fund this account with your money and then the artificial intelligence system will connect to this account but it will not have access to your money. It will just copy the traits. So you can withdraw that money anytime you like. You can stop copying the system anytime you like. And this is what I like the most with this system, because it gives you all the flexibility that you need. There is no some kind of subscription. Some are rules that you need to be in there for one year or whatever. You can just draw money whenever you like. If you need money or whatever.

**Robert Rolih:**

In case of artificial intelligence, do we get the interest to our account on a monthly or a yearly basis? It's basically on a daily basis. If there is a daily profit this will show immediately on your account.

**Robert Rolih:**

So, it's not like, because all the trading is done or on your account and this is short-term trading. All the traits are made for hours or maybe days.

**Robert Rolih:**

So this will get, profits are are made every day, and you will be seeing that all the time. So it's daily.

**Robert Rolih:**

For some people are asking about installments. Now, let me tell you that we didn't talk about that with Raymond. So, Henry and a couple of other people who are asking for installments, again, you will not be able to get the same offer as the others, but please send an email to the same email address that Raymond gave you earlier and we will try to find a solution.

**Raymond Aaron:**

Let me give it to you again. M as in mother. Mpatel. M as in mother. M-P-A-T-E-L @aaron.com. Aaron is of course, A-A-R-O-N. You can see it at the bottom of your screen, and you'll speak to my chief financial officer and he will offer you a payment plan over three months, four months, five months, whatever you need. Just talk to him. He's really good. He'll take very, very good care of you. mpatel@arron.com

**Robert Rolih:**

Then, what percent of your portfolio do you invest in the stock as to income builder? Approximately 10%. Approximately 10%. When you invest in any short term vehicle, you should be a bit more careful even though it's amazing it can produce a lot of returns and so on, but still this is short-term trading and you should be a bit more careful. And I teach about this in my course. So approximately 10% of my portfolio is in artificial intelligence trading.

**Robert Rolih:**

Is there a minimum investment for artificial intelligence? Yes, it's $3000. So, $3000 is the minimum.

**Raymond Aaron:**

That's really small. Wow.

**Robert Rolih:**

Yeah. Usually this kind of systems have like . . . I just, a couple of weeks ago, I talked with a team of traders from Israel that are trading with gold and they are having good returns, not as good as artificial intelligence, but they are having good returns.

**Robert Rolih:**

And when I asked them, because they wanted to cooperate with me, and asked them what was the minimum investment for the time and they said $100,000. $100,000, so I said, "Okay, it's okay. But for most of my clients, this will not be good, because they don't have $100,000 to put into a short-term trading product." So I said no.

**Robert Rolih:**

So can investing in index funds be done through Canadian RRSP or DFSA or is it separate? It can be done through that. You can invest in index funds through your pension plan.

**Robert Rolih:**

Does this offer include a copy of your book? I kept something even better, but this will be a surprise for you. So, when you buy this we will give you a surprise. I will not tell you what is it now, but it will be something even better than the copy of my book.

**Robert Rolih:**

Okay. Are you going to give us the list of index funds and the six you are investing? Yes, sure. So in the course, you will get the complete list. 14 index funds that are on my list and I will also tell you which one's I'm investing in. But I will also tell you that I'm very young. I'm 17 years old now. I'm 43. So I'm 43, and this selection or 16 index funds that I selected are working for me, so this works for me because I'm 43. But if you are 55 or if you are a bit more conservative than me, then you will need to make a different selection and I will lead you step-by-step through that. So my 16 index funds can be a good solution for somebody who is similar to me, because the similar age or similar goals, but for somebody who is a bit different, you will need to choose your own selection, but I will give you the solution. How to do it with the side-by-side strategy. And as you will see, it's very, very simple.

**Robert Rolih:**

Yes, ETF's are basically index funds. So ETFs are index funds. This is the same.

**Robert Rolih:**

What are your returns for the last five, 10 years or what do you expect your returns will be? So my returns for index funds are very, very good, because I started . . . But it's a very, it's a good question, but it's a question that is a tricky question. Because in the last 10 years, if you started to invest any time after the last financial crisis you are having amazing returns right now, even though the market has dropped now. So I'm still quite a lot in profit, but these are my long-term investments and I don't care what is going on in the short-term. I'm just looking for more buying opportunities right now.

**Robert Rolih:**

So my long term investments that have been making from the year 2010 to '12 and on, because at that time I learned about index funds and all these time I'm sharing now, I'm keeping them. I didn't sell them before this Covid crisis. Even though I thought and I shared this with my clients that the market is overvalued, but I said to them, whatever you bought in the last years just keep, because these are your long-term investments. You don't sell your long term investments, you are just looking for additional buying opportunities for new investments.

**Robert Rolih:**

So we are not speculating, we are investing for the long run and but of course, if there is an opportunity when you can get index funds very cheaply, then of course take it. And this is 2020. This is the opportunity.

**Robert Rolih:**

No. So, Craig, we never use covered calls or stock options and stuff like this for long-term investing to cover our profits and so on. This is, these products are short-term speculative products and most people who are playing with this product, they lose their money. So for smart, long-term investors, my strategy is something that will work and you will have no problems with it. You don't need to speculate and try to do whatever you proposed here, because most of the time if you try to speculate for the short run with these leverage products and so on, you will be losing money. So, no. We don't do that.

**Robert Rolih:**

Yeah. Artificial intelligence. One thing that I need to emphasize is if you are from Canada or if you are from anywhere else in the world, you will be able to use it. If you are from the United States, you will not be able to use it. United States has several laws that don't allow people to use this copy functions from other traders. And that is why artificial intelligence system is not available for United States investors. So if you are from United States, you will not be able to use artificial intelligence. But if, when you buy my course, I will give you something else that you will be able to use. So we will give you, so just write us an email after you buy this course and we will give you another thing. It's not like artificial intelligence, because Americans cannot use it, but it's a totally different thing. But it might be a good idea to increase our short term returns.

**Raymond Aaron:**

Can I just tell you something?

**Robert Rolih:**

Yeah.

**Raymond Aaron:**

Some of my clients texting me directly about this and one of them said, "Raymond, this guy is a legend." He apparently loved your [inaudible 00:19:36]. And another one of my clients said, "Not only that, I also bought his book." So they're loving you. This is amazing.

**Robert Rolih:**

Thank you. Thank you.

**Raymond Aaron:**

Wow.

**Robert Rolih:**

Thank you. I just hope that I gave some value today, even if you don't buy that you learned about these things, because the financial industry tries to take advantage of us and they are most of the time, most of them just think about one goal and that is how to take our money and put it into their pockets. And I lost a lot of money, because I trusted my financial advisors. I really, this was high six figures at the time.

**Robert Rolih:**

Can I use artificial intelligence from Slovakia? Daniella, yes you can. Slovakia is okay. Only United States is not allowed, but all the other countries are okay.

**Robert Rolih:**

No, it's not. ITVantage. So these solution for artificial intelligence trading is not public is just in invitation only. And only my client from London, she offers this to his clients. And now recently, I've started to offer this to my clients. But he wants to keep this as private as possible and he's only cooperating with me, because he old big couple of favors from the past. And we are good friends. So this is the only reason that I'm able to offer these also to my clients. And I also have a special limits, how many clients can I connect. But now, for this group, I think that there will be no problems because I have some space available. But sometimes, when I have very large groups, then I need to limit the number of people who can enter at any given month.

**Robert Rolih:**

If US citizen, can you use that artificial intelligence? Rochelle, I have no idea. That's probably a thing that if you are US and Canada citizen, you will need to ask the broker about that, if you can open the account or not, because they don't accept US clients, the broker that we are using. So you will need to check this with the broker later.

**Robert Rolih:**

Yeah, US and Canadian citizen. Really, I don't have it. We would need to ask the broker that.

**Robert Rolih:**

With artificial intelligence, all be doing the same sector or do you have to make selections? So artificial intelligence will not be trading with stocks. It is trading with Forex, so with currencies. So this is Forex market and gold. It's using gold and different currency pairs. So it's not connected in any way with index funds or the stock market.

**Robert Rolih:**

Can I have a special promo code, please? Yes, Andrea, you got it. So today, by the end of this day, you can get in the course for $997, so this is the special code for you. Okay, Raymond, I think that I went through all the questions.

**Raymond Aaron:**

Well, you not only did that you gave a dazzling presentation. I'm really moved. I knew how you were, but I had never heard your whole presentation from beginning to end. I'm deeply moved. You gave a long-term and a long-term high profit and a short-term high profit option and the financial literacy component, so that we can continue to grow in our wisdom and know what to do on our own. I'm really moved by it. And every one of my clients who joins, congratulations.

**Raymond Aaron:**

If you didn't join, there's a couple of reasons. Maybe you didn't join because you didn't have enough money. Hello? That's the problem. That's because you're working for a living and because you're spending all your money every single month and you don't have the financial literacy to save even $5. I'm not putting you down, I'm just saying that if you don't have the $997 it's because of your poor financial literacy.

**Raymond Aaron:**

Another reason is, you just might not be interested. You just want to play this lifetime and I get it. There's nothing wrong with that. But if you're interested at all in making these commitments to yourself and to your family, this is it. There is no better deal in the world. This is it.

**Raymond Aaron:**

And I'm honored, Robert, that you're my friend. I'm honored that we got together several years ago. I got a call out of the blue saying, hello, my name is Robert. I live in Slovenia. I never heard of Robert and I never heard of Slovenia, but I started to love that guy and now I totally love him. And I've been to Slovenia so many times now it's such a beautiful country, and Robert himself is a towering gentleman with lots of wisdom and he's giving it all to you in this program. So get into it. You've got today only. Thank you so much. You did a brilliant job. Thank you. Thank you. Thank you.

**Robert Rolih:**

Thank you. And just my last message. Investing is simple. It's just the financial industry that works hard to make it complex, so when you know the right details then everything will become simple. So purchase the course now and then we will be together for the long run and that will keep you updated and I will keep you in touch with me all the time and answer your question and so on.

**Robert Rolih:**

I'm working 24/7 for my clients. Can I just show you one email that I got?

**Raymond Aaron:**

Go ahead.

**Robert Rolih:**

Yeah, I hoped that I will be able to show that. Let me just go to my email. It's such an amazing email.

**Raymond Aaron:**

Just before you go, just before you go, please everyone take a screenshot so that you can see the website, aaron.com/moneymakingmachine. Please take a screenshot or take your cell phone and snap a photograph of it, if you haven't purchased it yet and you need another hour or so to figure it out, aaron.com/moneymakingmachine and if you need to contact my chief financial officer, M as in mother mpatel@aaron, A-A-R-O-N .com. Go ahead, let's see this email.

**Robert Rolih:**

I hoped that I would find it. Sorry, but I totally forgot the name of the client.

**Raymond Aaron:**

Just tell us we'll believe you.

**Robert Rolih:**

Yeah, he said something like this, that he works with a lot of experts and so on. He bought a lot of online courses and the live courses and so on. But recently when he sends a question to somebody, he doesn't get an answer, because I don't know, maybe it's because of the Covid problems or something else. But he said, very rarely I get an answer and I got the master familiar in one hour. Because basically I'm, in these times, I'm swamped with work, but I'm going through all the emails, all of my clients get my personal email because I'm sending everything, all the video we do seminars and everything I send from my personal email and they can ask me questions and so on. And I answer them in 24 hours you will get my answer usually much earlier. but he said, very rarely, and now I'm getting an answer to my questions, but you gave me an answer immediately and you are doing such a good job and so on.

**Robert Rolih:**

So this is something that I really . . . I know that my clients are the most important thing and I always think of them.

**Raymond Aaron:**

And you've taken care of me and you've taught my clients how to take care of themselves and their family. You're a real gentleman.

**Robert Rolih:**

Thank you.

**Raymond Aaron:**

Thank you. Thank you. Bye-bye everyone.

**Robert Rolih:**

And thank all of you who attended. Thank you, bye.

# Spirituality in the Face of Chaos

## Martin Rutte

**Raymond Aaron:**

He has recently written a book that he's been working on for 25 years, Project Heaven on Earth, which is also Project Heaven on Earth. He's also got a new idea that he's working on. He is amazingly the only person who was ever presented at the Harvard Business School four times. I'm honored to say he's been my friend for over three decades. We love each other. We are both members of the Transformational Leadership Council. He's one of the top transformational leaders in the world, and he's one of my dearest, dearest friends, Martin Rutte.

**Raymond Aaron:**

Nope, you have to unmute yourself. Unmute yourself. Press the mic.

**Martin Rutte:**

Ah, now can you hear me?

**Raymond Aaron:**

Yes, perfectly. We can hear you and we can see you.

**Martin Rutte:**

But I can't see you.

**Raymond Aaron:**

I know. It's some glitch in the system. You'll have to do [inaudible 00:00:59].

**Martin Rutte:**

Thank you for the introduction. Good to be with you all. And as Raymond said, my background is in corporate consulting, so I've spoken four times at the Harvard Business School, as he said, on vision. Some of my clients have included Marion Merrell Dow, Consumer Pharmaceuticals, Virgin Records, Sony Pictures, Southern California Edison. And my job with all of those folks was to talk about vision, to talk about where they want to go in the world. And about, as Raymond said, about 25, 30 years ago, I was thinking I'm not happy with what I'm seeing in the world. There's a lot of suffering. There's a lot of problems and ongoing sufferings that I don't think really need to be here. So what to do about that?

**Martin Rutte:**

And then one day I said, "Well, what about a vision for the world?" And I thought, "Hmm." And then this thought popped into my head, "You mean heaven on earth?" And I thought, "Oh my God, you can't say that." You can't talk about heaven on earth. I mean, people will think you're crazy. People will think you're some kind of religious zealot trying to impose some kind of nutty thing on people.

**Martin Rutte:**

But the more I thought about it, the more I thought, "But wait a minute, we can talk about hell on earth, can't we?" That's a permissible conversation. We see all the hells on earth that are going on, economic refugees, and no, I don't even need to talk about COVID. And so why can't we talk about the kind of world that we really want, the kind of life, the kind of work, the kind of nation, and the kind of world we want.

**Martin Rutte:**

And if we had a magic wand, and could just envision what heaven on earth is, wouldn't we want to kind of go into that arena and see what was there? So that began my going on this inquiry, and by inquiry, I mean, I started asking people, "What's heaven on earth for you? What's heaven on earth for you? What's heaven on earth for you?" I actually didn't even have an idea in my own mind about what it meant, but I was interested in discovery. And the way I discovered it is not by reading. The way I discover it is by just talking to people and asking questions.

**Martin Rutte:**

I'd love to ask the same question over and over and over and over again. In this case it was, "What's heaven on earth for you? What's heaven on earth for you?" And slowly over the years, as I began to investigate that topic, more and more of it became really clear to me, and it boiled down to three very simple questions. This was after hundreds and hundreds of interviews, I began to see that we could really help people get at what heaven on earth is for you.

**Martin Rutte:**

So I'm going to ask you these three questions. Let me just see if I have my little . . . I do. I am going to ask you these three questions. These questions are also available on my website, projectheavenonearth.com, but I'm going to ask them really slowly. I'd like you just to contemplate them and I'm assuming, Raymond, that if I ask the questions, I can see responses, and can I do that?

**Raymond Aaron:**

Martin?

**Martin Rutte:**

Yeah.

**Raymond Aaron:**

So Francis is going to be handling that because there are thousands of comments coming in. Also, I fault you considerably for leaving out an important point. You were an extremely successful seminar leader in Success Principles and a very successful consultant. And I being your best friend, you asked me if you should enter the spiritual realm of heaven on earth and I said, "Absolutely not, don't you dare." And that's the reason he did it. That's how wonderful friends we are.

**Martin Rutte:**

Whenever I go to Raymond with this idea about what I want to do in life and he says, "No, you can't do it," then that's the stamp of approval, go ahead and do it. So, thank you.

**Raymond Aaron:**

That's how good friends we are.

**Martin Rutte:**

That's how good . . . what I was talking about to you earlier I said we're brothers from different mothers and different fathers, but our progeny is irrelevant. We're together. So here are my three heaven on earth questions and, Francis, I'd love some feedback if you get it. Question one, recall a time when you experienced heaven on earth, recall a time when you experienced heaven on earth. Can we get some feedback on that? Anybody typing a message?

**Francis:**

Now, Martin, I will share with you, there is a slight delay. So they might take a minute before they hear your answer.

**Martin Rutte:**

All right.

**Raymond Aaron:**

And I will give my answer while the delay goes on.

**Martin Rutte:**

Thanks.

**Raymond Aaron:**

And it will sound sucky. It will sound sucky. But every single time I see Karyn when I haven't seen her even for an hour, like if she leaves the home and comes back, every single time I run to the door to see her, heaven on earth for me is that I am married to Karyn.

**Martin Rutte:**

And I see the love between you. We did that onesie report other night, which was hysterical. So I do see that. Yeah. Francis, is there a comment?

**Francis:**

Yes. Christina says, "I took a retreat called Peace Awareness Training."

**Martin Rutte:**

Thank you. I'm going to come back to the answers in a moment. Thank you, Christina. Anyone else?

**Francis:**

Michael, "I wanted to go home from being a refugee." Luciana, "Every time I meditate." Josephine, "I was visited by my nephew after he passed and he gave me a message for our family."

**Martin Rutte:**

Whoa.

**Francis:**

I hope I've pronounced that correct, "When I'm on the beaches of Aruba."

**Martin Rutte:**

So notice what happens, folks. I've asked that question and the responses come in. I'm going to go into more depth on each of those. So question one, recall a time when you experienced heaven on earth, what was going on? Question two, imagine you have a magic wand. If you have a pen or pencil in your hand right now, you have a magic wand, and with it, you can have heaven on earth. All you have to do is wave it, and you can have heaven on earth. What is heaven on earth for you? So Raymond, you want to answer that while we're waiting for the responses.

**Raymond Aaron:**

The delay is going on. Heaven on earth for me is everybody doing what they love for their work, everybody the book, double your income, doing what you love. And heaven on earth for me would be everybody doing what they love and earning abundantly. There'd be no war if that was the case. Everybody would be happy and earning abundantly.

**Martin Rutte:**

Let me just do one little correction. Change the word would to is.

**Raymond Aaron:**

Everyone is doing exactly what they want, earning abundantly and there is no war because everyone's happy.

**Martin Rutte:**

Fabulous. Francis, anyone else?

**Francis:**

Jeanette, "My heaven on earth was growing up with our family on our farm, 400 acres." "Financial freedom." Christina, "Staying tuned to myself full of love and lights."

**Martin Rutte:**

Is there a wonderful end?

**Raymond Aaron:**

Francis is good. He can figure out how to come back on. Nope, we've lost your sound, Martin. We've lost your sound. Francis, can you bring Martin's sound back on?

**Francis:**

Yes.

**Martin Rutte:**

We take, in the next 24 hours. There we go, we're back. All right. Any other answers?

**Francis:**

Peaceful relationships with Josephine. Mary is, "No evil." Luciana, "Everybody [inaudible 00:08:50] purpose. "Heaven on earth." [Inaudible 00:08:53]

**Martin Rutte:**

Say that again.

**Francis:**

Everyone's finding their own purpose. Larissa, "Heaven on earth, do what you love to do, financial security and helping people."

**Martin Rutte:**

Lovely. Let's go to the third question. What simple, easy, concrete step, what simple, easy, concrete step will you take in the next 24 hours to have more of that heaven on earth? Raymond, do you want to answer that while we're waiting?

**Raymond Aaron:**

Well, for me, it's a giant step. I created this 14-hour, 10,000 participant, mega-teleseminar with 19 world famous authors. That's my little step, but also, do you know what? I am sequestered with my darling wife and cat, and I love going up and just petting her. And the instant I walked towards her, she starts purring.

**Martin Rutte:**

You mean, your wife or the cat? Who's the she?

**Karyn:**

Both of us.

**Raymond Aaron:**

And even though I'm only helping one entity, and it's a cat, I am so uplifted. And so I think that my upliftment because I'm petting my cat and enjoying her purring, will spread to the world.

**Martin Rutte:**

Yes. Lovely. Francis, other answers.

**Francis:**

Yes. "Open up to yourself." Luciano, "Write about conscious existence." Michael, "Read the Bible."

**Raymond Aaron:**

Oh, wow.

**Francis:**

Larisa, "Continue to do what I'm doing. I live heaven on earth. Thank you Lord." Vanessa, "Practicing and receiving being open."

**Martin Rutte:**

Fabulous. Fabulous. I'm always touched, I got to tell you. I'm always touched when people share what heaven on earth is for them.

**Raymond Aaron:**

It didn't specify which Testament of the Bible.

**Martin Rutte:**

All right, answer which Testament, which chapter? So the three questions. Let me go through them one by one and this, again, is on projectheavenonearth.com. One, recall a time when you experienced heaven on earth. I want you to notice that what you did was answer the question. What you did not do, and what no one does is ask what do you mean by heaven on earth? So how do you know what I'm talking about? I never even defined the term heaven on earth. And, yet, for those of you who answered, you knew instantly what I was talking about. And it's because of what I call . . . you have what's called an already knowing about what heaven on earth is. And when I ask, "Recall a time when you experienced heaven on earth," you go right to that experience and, boom, there it is. It's present. And the only way you can do that is if you know what heaven on earth is. That's the already knowing.

**Martin Rutte:**

Second question, recall a time when you experienced heaven on . . . Excuse me, here's a magic wand, and with it, you can have heaven on earth. What's heaven on earth for you? The reason I put the magic wand in is to remove the necessity of having to know how you're going to do it. And if you don't have to know how you're going to do it, you go right to the what and we heard some beautiful, beautiful answers there, beautiful answers. I'm always touched when I do a webinar or a live seminar, how people know instantly what heaven on earth is for them. And so this work, this book is designed to bring that into conscious awareness and action, and so the action becomes the third step.

**Martin Rutte:**

Third question, what simple, easy, concrete step will I take in the next 24 hours? I don't want to leave heaven on earth up here, which is lovely. I want to ground it in simple action. One of the things that I've learned over the years is the power of that word simple because if you think in your mind it's too big, you'll stop. However, if it's something simple, well, I can do that. Well then you start doing it, and the movement begins. Any other questions before I continue, Francis . . . or Raymond?

**Martin Rutte:**

Okay, so let me talk about what happened so far in terms of the effectiveness. As Raymond said, I started about 35 years ago doing this, putting this out, putting this out, putting this out. It was a dream that came to me. It was something I knew I had to do, and I started by declaration. I'll explain. The way you start a new story in your life, or in your business, or in your nation, or in the world is by declaring it. So I said, "I'm going to help experience and co-create heaven on earth in the world."

**Martin Rutte:**

How? I don't know. Let me just start. Let me just see what the next step is, and the next step, and the next step. That's the way you can begin to begin co-creating heaven on earth in the world. Whatever that dream was when I waved the magic wand and said, "What is heaven on earth for you using this magic wand," it's time, with your permission, to have that start to come out in the world. It's time, at a larger level . . . this is really what this work is about, is that we're experiencing and we're co-creating the new story of what it means to be a human, and what it means to be humanity. And what a perfect time to do this.

**Martin Rutte:**

I remember years ago, as Raymond said, when I started to do some work in spirituality and work, I went to an Anglican Bishop in Toronto, God rest his soul, Bishop Henry Hill, and I said, "You know, part of what I want to do is I want to just go on a little retreat for a year." So we sold our business, and we sold our home, and I went up north in North Toronto for a year and kind of thought about what was next. And I said, "Henry, I'm going on retreat."

**Martin Rutte:**

And he said, "Okay, there's three elements of retreat." And I'm saying this in the larger context of what I believe is happening in the world today. Corona has forced us into retreat from the normal way we operate in life. So the first thing that you do in retreat is withdraw. We watched a lot of television, a lot of shows that I've been wanting to see. I really didn't have a lot of energy for work. That's stage one. Stage two is renewal, and I can feel it. Raymond, I listened to some of the presenters today, Jack and Mark Victor Hansen and I think, Francis, and it . . . fabulous. I mean, I got even more juiced. And so I've been thinking about what the next level of my work is as well.

**Martin Rutte:**

So there's this sense of renewal, and pretty soon we'll go into the final stage, which is return. We will return to the world with a new sense of being, a new sense of perspective. Isn't this then the perfect time to begin to consider the kind of world that we deeply want? My suggestion is yes, it is, and the way to do that is by you saying, "Okay, I'm in. I'm going to help co-create an experience heaven on earth."

**Martin Rutte:**

And so Raymond talked about . . . well, you can see my book below, Project Heaven on Earth. It's on Amazon. And what's interesting is the first word. If you notice, you look down, it says Project Heaven on Earth. Well, we all know what a project is. It's the noun. You and I are doing something, but it's also the verb to project heaven on earth. We're projecting our being of heaven on earth into our world.

**Martin Rutte:**

So the world starts to line up with our deep soul's longing for the kind of world that we truly want. I don't want COVID. I don't want massive poverty. I don't want the refugee situation. I want those to end. I remember years ago a guy wrote a book called The End of Poverty. It was the first time I'd ever heard of anyone or seen anyone write a book about ending a suffering in the world. That's the kind of stuff that we want to do with Heaven on Earth.

**Martin Rutte:**

So I started . . . I distill these three questions. I went and I started asking people the three questions that I just asked you. And what began to emerge for me was what I call the gateways into heaven on earth. The same arenas of answers kept coming up over and over and over. So the rest of the book goes into those, what are those gateways . . . inner. There are people who say the way you create heaven on earth is to create it inside. The more it's in here, the more it can be expressed out in the world.

**Martin Rutte:**

There are those people who live a global value. My wife's global value is joy. When she walks into a room, joy is present. She wants joy in the world. There are those people who say it's outer. The way you create heaven on earth is to end the suffering, end war, end poverty, end the refugee situation, end sexual slavery, end poverty.

**Martin Rutte:**

There are people who are taking on their entire nation. I have a woman in Austria, Elizabeth, who said to me . . . I said, Elizabeth, what's your project?" And she said, "Austria is a heaven on earth nation." And I went, "Woah, why do you say that?" And she said, in her halting English, "Well, Martin, because it's simple." And she taught me the relevance and the importance of the word simple because whatever is simple to you, that's what you do. One of the guys in one of Raymond's courses, Charles, has created a new Facebook group called Africa, A Heaven on Earth Continent. That was incredible to me.

**Martin Rutte:**

Another one gentlemen from one of Raymond's courses, is getting his PhD in heaven on earth. We have a man, a police officer who you'll hear on this show, World Prosper Summit, Justin Criner, who wrote a 28-page manual called Heaven on Earth for Law Enforcement. There are people on Prince Edward Island who are spending the summer who declared Prince Edward Island is Canada's first heaven on earth province. Two summers ago, I interviewed all four political party leaders in this province, including the premier, and they all talked about what heaven on earth is for them.

**Martin Rutte:**

Another example, a real estate agent in Halifax, Brenda MacKenzie. Her suffering in the world, homelessness. You could see how deeply, deeply, deeply that hurt her. Her project, a home for everyone. She went back to her real estate agent and got each of the agents to agree that with every house sold, a hundred dollars would automatically come off their commission check. They all said yes, happy to do that. They've raised over $400,000 in the last four years.

**Martin Rutte:**

Another example, a woman in Lunenburg was crazed about violence against women. She'd been to the police, she'd been to the province, nothing, nothing, nothing. "What would you do, Martin?" "Well," I said, "I don't know your situation financially. You could donate $5,000. You could donate a penny." "Well, what difference would a penny make?" One of the other women on the call said, "But wait a minute. What if everybody in your county donated a penny a day to help end violence against women?"

**Martin Rutte:**

She started a program called Making Change, in which they handed out a little Mason Jar with a sign with a picture of a woman, half her face beaten up, half her face bright alive, and they asked people, get this, to donate a penny a day for a year. You couldn't put a check in it for $3.65, a penny a day, a day, a day, a day. They raised $2,500. They took that to the government of Canada, Status of Women, who gave them a hundred thousand dollars for each of the subsequent three years based on that little idea. What difference will a penny a day make?

**Martin Rutte:**

So, by reading this book, by going through it, what you'll discover is what your project is that's simple for you. You'll find a gateway. The book is full of examples, and stories, and inspiring quotes, and each of the gateways that I mentioned plus . . . Now here's what I'm asking you to do. I would like you to buy three of these books. They're on Amazon, easy to get, Project Heaven on Earth. Buy three, one for you, one for somebody in your life right now . . . just take a second, who's that person who would benefit most from getting a copy of this book? Okay, that person. And the third one is for somebody who will be coming into your life that you don't know right now, and you'll be able to hand that to them.

**Martin Rutte:**

And so then you'll be able to be an ambassador of heaven on earth, an agent of heaven on earth, or an angel of heaven on earth, and impact the world because you started by saying, "My job here is to help co-create and experience heaven on earth."

**Martin Rutte:**

Raymond questions, we've got what, six minutes to go? I'm happy to go on, but any questions have come in? So projectheavenonearth.com, Project Heaven on Earth on Amazon.

**Raymond Aaron:**

Yeah. I just realized again why I love you so much.

**Martin Rutte:**

Because I have you as a friend?

**Raymond Aaron:**

And my wife. Now you gave such a sweet, soft, presentation. Everyone else gave hard-hitting, watch out for this, be careful of that, you can succeed, and you just want to bring heaven on earth because it's already here. So it's really an unveiling, not a bringing.

**Martin Rutte:**

Correct.

**Raymond Aaron:**

Wow.

**Martin Rutte:**

Let me tell you one way that I know. If you go to Google and put in the phrase, heaven on earth, in quotes 2018 and put the same phrase, heaven on earth in quotes 2019, and then heaven on earth in quotes 2020 on Google. What you'll see roughly in 2018 was about 6.7 million or 6.6 million results, not all mine. Last year, it was 11.2, an 82% rise and the last time I checked it, about two or three weeks ago, we were already at 7.7 million for this year.

**Martin Rutte:**

So it's coming in powerfully, and when you think of it, it makes sense because of the hells on earth that we see now, isn't it more appropriate to begin to think about the post-Corona era, the new PC, and begin to put into place the kind of world we want. This is our time. Raymond.

**Raymond Aaron:**

Thank you for bringing light to the world. Thank you for bringing light to me and my clients. Thank you for . . . you mentioned one of my clients decided to do his PhD. This is such a wonderful story. He's a gentleman just before retirement, and he gave up on his PhD five years ago. He did 95% of it, but he gave up because he didn't have a compelling topic for his dissertation. And he didn't want to just do it on anything just to get a PhD, and he was sad. And when he heard your presentation at my event, he said, "That's it." I'm going to be the first heaven on earth PhD.

**Martin Rutte:**

That's right.

**Raymond Aaron:**

He has gone back to his university. They've allowed him to restart his PhD, and they've approved the topic heaven on earth. And so Martin and I and many people we know are going to be dancing at his PhD graduation ceremony. We will be there.

**Martin Rutte:**

> My mind is already boggled by the . . . we have a doctor, PhD. And what about Charles doing Africa is a Heaven on Earth Continent.

**Raymond Aaron:**

> You produced enormous results in your lifetime. You're a wonderful guy.

**Martin Rutte:**

> Thank you. I love you, and I love Karen, and I love the pussycat. What's the pussycat's name?

**Raymond Aaron:**

> Friendly.

**Martin Rutte:**

> I have to tell you, I got three minutes. I have to tell you, Steven Wright, you know, the comedian?

**Raymond Aaron:**

> Yeah.

**Martin Rutte:**

> He named his dog, Stay. So he says to his dog, "Come, Stay."

**Raymond Aaron:**

> And the poor dog doesn't know what to do.

**Martin Rutte:**

> Exactly.

**Raymond Aaron:**

And so if he comes, it's okay, and if he stays it's okay.

**Martin Rutte:**

Yeah, he's in therapy. He's in therapy, dog therapy.

**Raymond Aaron:**

The dog is in therapy?

**Martin Rutte:**

No.

**Raymond Aaron:**

So, Francis, if you don't come up with a question, Martin and I are just going to laugh for the remaining few minutes.

**Martin Rutte:**

We've got three minutes.

**Francis:**

We have a few questions. Lots of thank you's. We have magnifique, lots of thank you's, Martin, amazing, amazing information. We have a question. Can you repeat the three questions you gave earlier?

**Martin Rutte:**

Yeah. Easier. Go to projectheavenonearth.com and you'll see them there.

**Francis:**

Perfect. Let's see-

**Raymond Aaron:**

Projectheavenonearth.com.

**Francis:**

We have a question from Mary, if I can find it. We had a lot of questions come in. Just a second, okay, "What if I want to start a Memorial Annual Giving Fund to help others? Will this work?"

**Martin Rutte:**

Sure. If the context that you hold it in is, and this is my contribution to heaven on earth, yes.

**Raymond Aaron:**

Wonderful.

**Martin Rutte:**

Is there another question?

**Raymond Aaron:**

I have no idea what you meant by that, but it sounded really spiritual.

**Martin Rutte:**

Well, so she's creating this memorial fund, okay. And she's going to do that anyway. In addition, she could also say I'm creating and doing this memorial fund, and it is also my contribution to heaven on earth.

**Raymond Aaron:**

Oh, I see. Okay. Good. Francis.

**Martin Rutte:**

Francis, another question?

**Francis:**

Very great presentation. I have a, "Hello Martin," from Patty and Steve Harris, "love you."

**Raymond Aaron:**

Great.

**Martin Rutte:**

Hello.

**Francis:**

We have, "Where to follow you?" So your website, project on . . .

**Martin Rutte:**

Projectheavenonearth.com.

**Francis:**

Perfect. "Martin, you're amazing, thank you." "Thanks, Martin. Great as always." Lots of accolades. No questions that I see though.

**Raymond Aaron:**

Hold on a second. I'm on for seven hours. Martin's on for half an hour and they want to follow him.

**Martin Rutte:**

I'm sorry my sound is off, Raymond.

**Raymond Aaron:**

Well, they loved you.

**Martin Rutte:**

You have smart attendees, what can I say.

**Raymond Aaron:**

I see. Well, Martin, I love you. You did a brilliant job.

**Martin Rutte:**

Thank you.

**Raymond Aaron:**

You've been an oasis of spirituality and gentleness, and insights, and thoughtfulness amid this Coronavirus lockdown and amidst this seven hours today of wisdom from all the other masters. Thank you.

**Martin Rutte:**

Thank you, dear brother. Thank you, Karen. Thank you, Friendly. Thanks, everybody.

# Being Calm & Centered During Troubled Times

## Hale Dwoskin

**Raymond Aaron:**

Hale is helping you recover from your emotional scars of the past. He teaches the Sedona method for decades. He's world famous for it. That's why he was in the movie The Secret and just before he starts, I want to remind you that it's an extra special bonus with no strings attached, no obligation, but it's an unbelievable bonus. My team of four coaches is giving you half hour coaching session for free. You just go to Aaron.com A A R O N. Aaron.com/coachingsession, singular. Coaching session, one word, aaron.com/coachingsession. And you register on the calendar for any time period you want 12 hours a day for seven days starting Sunday and you will get an honest half hour coaching session of what's the next step for you or anything that you wish to discuss on any one of the speakers. So, Hale, my dear friend, are you here?

**Raymond Aaron:**

I can see you on the panelist. Just unmute yourself. Hale, click the mic or maybe Francis can do it for you.

**Hale Dwoskin:**

Yeah, I think Francis just did it.

**Raymond Aaron:**

Good. Hale, all my dear friend.

**Hale Dwoskin:**

How are you?

**Raymond Aaron:**

I'm so happy I haven't seen you in ages, but I love you. I love hugging you. I love how simple your program is and how many people it deeply helps. And please, I want to hear your message again and I want my wonderful clients to hear your message again of how they can clean up and eliminate their scars from the past and move ahead of their inhibitions and embarrassments and all that crap-ola to move forward.

**Hale Dwoskin:**

Okay, well I'll do that. So, hi everybody. So basically I want to take a step back. Scars. Does that sound a little boomy? Do I need to turn this down a little?

**Raymond Aaron:**

No, you're perfect.

**Hale Dwoskin:**

Okay, great. So basically right now, right here, you're already whole. You're already complete. You're already enough as you are, and right within you is the source of all joy, all power, all happiness, all knowingness. And it is already here now and we don't always see that because we're looking away from it.

And you can learn a very simple and powerful way to let go of whatever it is that's preventing you from living that moment to moment. And the reason it's easy to let go, or the reason you can learn that is because we all have a natural ability to let go of the thoughts, the feelings, the beliefs, the ideas, anything inside of us that's holding us back or keeping us stuck in any way.

**Hale Dwoskin:**

And it's something that you can do even when literally the shit is hitting the fan. Although hopefully you've never actually experienced shit hitting a fan. But when the world is in turmoil, that center of what you are, that being-ness is still always available and is easy to uncover if you're open to it. So how do you do that?

**Hale Dwoskin:**

How do you do that? By just allowing yourself to explore both that which you truly are and let go of everything else. And since everyone's into pens, I'll use a pen too. Although mine isn't as pretty as Martin's. Just an ordinary pen. And I think Raymond's was very pretty too. But anyway, I want you to know what I mean by letting go because sometimes we have all these beliefs about letting go and they're completely inaccurate. And that the biggest belief that most of us have is that it's difficult, that it takes time, a lot of time, and that we have to re-experience the trauma from the past or the problems from the past, but that couldn't be further from the truth.

**Hale Dwoskin:**

Right here, right now you have this natural ability to let go. And an example of it, if you can allow yourself to remember the last time you had a really good belly laugh, maybe you were laughing along with Martin and Raymond a minute ago or something someone said or did, or you watched a funny movie. But when you laugh, you're actually letting go to some degree. The more genuine the laughter is, the deeper the release, the deeper the letting go. Another time where we let go is when we just decide to. Everyone listening to me has been in a situation where a feeling was really disturbing them and they were still able to let go. And when they were able to let go, what that did is it changed the whole dynamic.

**Hale Dwoskin:**

We all actually do that when our back is against the wall, when we feel like there's nothing else, we can do about it. And children do this naturally. When you watch young children, you can see they'll have a knockdown, drag out fight with their friend, their best friend. And then all of a sudden, five or 10 minutes go by and they're fine. It's like nothing ever happened there. The kids are playing together again as though absolutely nothing has happened because nothing has. And so kids do this naturally and what happens is we train them out of it. People are telling us to sit down and shut up, do this, don't do that. And all that trains us out of that natural ability. And another example of watching children let go, have you ever been around a young child who falls down or hurts themselves in some way and then looks around to see if they need to be upset?

**Hale Dwoskin:**

And if they don't catch anyone's eye, there's no upset. Catch your eye I someone else's eye and all of a sudden, Oh my God, it's terrible. Please kiss it. You kiss it, they let go. So we can learn to do that natural letting go again, because it's our natural ability. And what happens when you let go is you open yourself to that infinite love and compassion and power and peace and certainty that's right within you. And you feel it immediately. You start to feel better immediately. And it also clears your mind so that you can see what needs to be done in life. Often, we are confused or uncertain about what to do next, especially right now. And part of that is because we're reacting to all the craziness. We're lost in the story of the coronavirus. Yet even then, you can step back inside and let go.

**Hale Dwoskin:**

And when you let go, the whole world opens up to you. And more importantly, you find that you feel relaxed, secure, open at home, wherever you are, even if you're sheltering at home. And so letting go is natural. And, but most of us as adults, you can't do it on call. We've forgotten how to do letting go. And once you get re-in-touch with it, then it becomes naturally available to you moment to moment throughout the day. And so if you just heard something on the news that really is upsetting, you can let go and then relax and have a good rest of the day. Or if you're trying to figure out what to do with your life now, since everything has changed, you can let go and you'll start to have the clarity of how to move forward. And also, you've been learning a lot today of all the things you should be doing or could be doing to transform your life.

**Hale Dwoskin:**

And you'll be learning more after I'm done and tomorrow too. But the thing that stops us often from pursuing what we know is best for us is our beliefs that we can't do it, that we don't know how, the fear, the uncertainty, the hold back. Imagine what would happen if any time that started to hold you back, you could just let that go as well. And that's really possible for you. And I'm not just saying that based on theory. I've been doing this work over 40 some odd years since 1976. So I think that's 46 years and I've seen hundreds of thousands of people all over the world let go of things that they thought would be absolutely impossible to let go of. I've seen them let go and totally transform their relationships, even the ones that they thought were unsavable. I've seen them let go and totally transform their health and wellbeing.

**Hale Dwoskin:**

I've seen people let go and it creates amazing abundance even in challenging times. And I've had that be my direct experience over and over and over and over again. And so what do I mean by letting go? I've been using that term a lot. So now to the pen. So pick up a pen or a pencil or a coin or paperclip, something you'd be willing to wet. Put the object in your hand and then grip it really tightly. Now, if you did this long enough, it would start to feel really uncomfortable and really familiar. Now your hand in this analogy, stop gripping. Your hand in this analogy represents your gut or your awareness. And the object represents all your unwanted feelings, your thoughts, your beliefs, your ideas, all the memories, everything inside of you. And Raymond mentioned trauma, but that's just a small piece of it.

**Hale Dwoskin:**

Most of us have some traumas, but we have all this other excess baggage that we're carrying around. It's actually like a huge sack we're carrying over our back. Well, when we're gripping this tightly, we can forget that it's not attached to us. It's even in our language. When we feel angry, what do we usually say? I'm angry. When we feel sad, what do we usually say? I'm sad. But are you actually the sadness? No, of course not. Are you actually the anger? No, of course not. But sometimes it feels that way. But every emotion that you have, even the ones that are most justified are as attached to you is this object is attached to your hand. So now roll it around in your hand. Obviously, it's not attached, is it? Is this object attached to your hand? No. And because it's not attached to your hand, those things actually also are not attached to you.

**Hale Dwoskin:**

So do this. Turn your hand upside down and just drop the object. That's how easy it can be to let go of even the most uncomfortable, the most traumatic experience or feeling or idea. Now that might seem over-simplistic and part of the power of the Sedona method is how simple and powerful it is. When we first started talking about letting go in the early seventies, almost no one else was talking about it except the 12-step program. Now everyone talks about letting go and how important it is. Yet, most people still find that the Sedona method is really the Rolls Royce for how to be able to do that effectively. We have many copiers, many, many over the years. And actually, I'm fine with that because I want this to get out to the world because think of how our world would be if everyone was letting go even a little more.

**Hale Dwoskin:**

And I want to make sure you're clear about this. When you're letting go, you're not letting go of your intuitive knowingness. You're not letting go of your natural innate intelligence. You're just letting go of that which is in the way. And the more you do that, the more you feel in control, the more you respond appropriately, the more you'll feel like you can have, be, or do anything you choose. So let's do a process. I'm going to give, if we have time, several processes during this half an hour because I want you to come away with something that you can use from now on. And this isn't obviously, I can't teach the entire Sedona method in a half an hour. Our audio program is 20 hours long and we have a 432 page book. So if I could summarize it, all of it in and a half hour, actually I would because I just feel it's so important, especially now. But I'm going to give you as much as I can in the time we have.

**Hale Dwoskin:**

So the first process we're going to do, and by the way, you don't need to do this outload. In our seminars, you don't have to ever share anything of a personal nature because it's not about the story. Many tools say you have to get really into the past experiences that have held you back, but you don't need to do that to let go. It's actually much more available than that. That's completely unnecessary. So the questions we're going to use for the first process are, could you let it go? Just could you, and if you were able to drop that pen or you could imagine dropping an object, then I know you can.

**Hale Dwoskin:**

The next question is, would you? And would you just mean are you willing to, and if you're ever trying this on your own and you're feeling a little unwilling, you can ask yourself, would I rather hold onto this feeling? Or would I rather have my goal and be free? Usually the answer is quite obvious. And if for right now you want to hold on, that's always fine. This is just a choice. It's never something that has to be forced. And the last question is when? And when is an invitation to decide to do it now. And it's really just a decision.

**Hale Dwoskin:**

So let's do the process together. So allow yourself to think of something you'd like to change or improve in your life right now. You can include the situation in the world or anything personal and just focus on that situation. And then in this moment, could you just allow or welcome or be present with whatever is being felt? The sensations, the feeling. Could you just let that be here for a moment? And then as best you can just for now, could you let it go? Just could you.

**Hale Dwoskin:**

Would you? When? Now you may have let go a little on the could you, you may have let go a little on the would you. You may have let go on the when. You may have let go on all three and you also may be wondering what's this all about? It may not have a fully resonated yet. But just as we go through this process, we're going to go through it a couple more times. As we go through this, do your best to allow yourself to feel more than think about it. And avoid debate. Just answer the question, yes or no. And no actually is a completely acceptable answer. I've met people in seminars scream, no, and still let go. So just be honest with yourself. I'd also ask that heart of awareness, that power within you, whether or not you can let go.

**Hale Dwoskin:**

If you ask the feeling, especially if you've gotten very identified or contracted around it, the feeling most often will say no. So make sure you're asking yourself, not the feeling. So again, allow yourself to focus and that same thing or anything else in your life that you'd like to change or improve. And then could you welcome whatever that stirs up inside of you? Could you just let it be here? And then could you welcome too? Or could you just be with it? And then as best you can, just for now, could you let it go? Just could you? Would you? When?

**Hale Dwoskin:**

Now you probably felt it a little more that time. So let's do it one more time. So in this moment, again, focus on that same thing or anything else in your life right now that you're wanting to change or improve, that you wish were different than the way it is. And could you just allow or be present with whatever that stirs up inside of you? Could you even welcome it? And then as best you can, just for now, could you let it go? Just could you? Would you? When?

**Hale Dwoskin:**

Now notice how you feel inside. Notice how more expanded or relaxed you feel. And that was just a few minutes. So just to review, you focus on whatever the issue is in the moment. You allow yourself to feel whatever you're feeling and just the allowing often is enough to make a difference because generally we're doing this with our feelings. No, I don't want to feel that, it's awful, if it's uncomfortable. But if you just do this. If you just open to it, then that in and of itself will often cause it to either relax completely or somewhat.

**Hale Dwoskin:**

And if the next question is, could you let it go? Just could you? The next question is, would you? The last question is, when? Now I know that sounds really simplistic and part of the reason it's as powerful as it is is because it's so simple. If you think about it, if young children can do this naturally, they don't even ask these questions. We as adults need to dumb it down and start with questions. Children just let go. People who are very content just let go and people who are very focused just let go. That's how they're able to go from one test to the other with such ease because they've learned to just let things go.

Now, not everyone does that of course. What most of us are doing all the time with our emotions, especially if they're really uncomfortable is we do this. We suppress them. Or we do this. We express them.

**Hale Dwoskin:**

But the balancing point between expression and suppression is right in between. And that's letting go and it's natural. And I've seen people just with that first baby step of the Sedona method, let go of fears and phobias. There was someone who had bridge that they had an accident on, so they avoided it. And it caused their commute to be three times as long as it needed to be.

**Hale Dwoskin:**

And they just did this part of the method, and the reason I know they just did this part is years ago we used to send out a DVD of me at a Jack Canfield seminar where I taught just this piece of the Sedona method. And the people would report all sorts of benefits just from that. In fact, they got so much from that they didn't always necessarily feel like they needed to go on. And what happened is just from practicing it, along with the DVD and with themselves, in just a short period of time, they were riding on the bridge as though nothing had happened. They didn't suppress it. They let it go. And there's so many examples of that. There are so many people that had their lives transformed just from that free gift that we were giving away.

**Hale Dwoskin:**

So think about your life. Are there things in your life that you wish you could let go of? Are there things within the way you think, the way you feel that you wish you could let go of? Are there things that you'd like to have more of? More money, for instance. Most people want that, especially right now. Well, again, when you let go, it clears the runway, it opens the field of possibility. And it allows that power that's at our core to shine through and help us create whatever is going to be the most useful or most helpful to us.

**Hale Dwoskin:**

And so, I don't know how to ask for questions, but I know there's an assistant there. Just before I go onto the next point, I just want to check if there are any questions about what I've covered so far. But while I'm doing that, I'll go on to the next point. So when you let go, you'll find that your mind gets clearer, your heart feels more open, and you feel more centered. Would you like more of that in your life? I bet you would.

**Hale Dwoskin:**

So another way of letting go is something we call triple welcoming. And it's focusing . . . Actually, before I do that, I'm going to talk a little bit about the five ways of letting go. The first way of letting go run back to the pen analogy, but you don't need to pick up a pen for this. So the first way is just to drop it. The second way is if you went through life open, allowing any feeling that you had in the moment would naturally roll through your consciousness. So the more allowing, the more open you are, to whatever you're experiencing inside, the less it sticks. And it's like water rolling off a duck's back or clouds floating through the sky or waves on the top of the ocean. If from the perspective of the ocean, when you really are welcoming and are open to what you're experiencing, does the ocean mind if there are waves?

**Hale Dwoskin:**

> If you were the ocean, you'd probably think they were cute. If you thought at all of course. Or if you were the sky and clouds were passing through, would that be upsetting? Of course not. Well, as you allow yourself to just open to your inner experience, allow it or welcome or be present with it, that in and of itself is a powerful way of letting go. Another way of letting go is without realizing it, we're always living life on the surface. We're seeing just the thinnest layer at the top, but if you allow yourself to dive into any emotion, it may slightly intensify at first. But if you go a little deeper, what you discover is that underneath all the turmoil, underneath all the suffering, underneath all the drama there is light. There's peace. There is certainty. But you never need to take my word for it. You can actually discover this from your own direct experience. So the third way of letting go is just diving into the feeling.

**Raymond Aaron:**

> Hale?

**Hale Dwoskin:**

> Yes?

**Raymond Aaron:**

> Hale, you've done a brilliant job. That comments are filled with, what a master. He's so calm. How can I follow him? I love his ideas on and on. They're just blowing up. You've done just a beautiful job of calming people in such a time of turmoil. I knew that you could do it, but you've actually done it brilliantly. Your voice is so calm. Your method is so calming. People have learned how to let go of that darn pen from their hand. You're brilliant already.

**Hale Dwoskin:**

Wow. I'm already out of time. I didn't even notice.

**Raymond Aaron:**

Yes.

**Hale Dwoskin:**

Oh wow.

**Raymond Aaron:**

Do you know what? I started at 11:00 AM Eastern and it is now 5:00 PM Eastern. It's been six straight hours and I can't even believe it. It just gone by so fast. You and all the other speakers were so fascinating. Hale, I can't wait to see you again.

**Hale Dwoskin:**

Likewise.

**Raymond Aaron:**

I can't wait to [crosstalk 00:31:09] when we're allowed to hug again.

**Hale Dwoskin:**

That'd be good. Hey, if people want information . . .

**Raymond Aaron:**

Please.

**Hale Dwoskin:**

Just go to sedona.com and if you go to sedona.com/prosper, we're giving away a free hour and eight minute movie.

**Raymond Aaron:**

Really?

**Hale Dwoskin:**

Yes. So it's the movie . . .

**Raymond Aaron:**

Sedonamethod.com/prosper.

**Hale Dwoskin:**

No, no. Just Sedona.com.

**Raymond Aaron:**

Sorry. Sedona.com. Sedona.com/prosper and he's doing something special out of respect for World Prosper Summit, which I didn't realize. Thank you so much. A free one hour and eight minute video. Sedona.com/prosper. Thank you. You're so generous. You're so calm. You're so sweet. You're so happy. I love you all over again.

**Hale Dwoskin:**

Likewise. Thanks Raymond.

# Financial First Aid Kit

## Loral Langemeier

**Raymond Aaron:**

Another superstar of the movie The Secret. The woman who is aptly named the millionaire maker, because when you are a client of hers, she hangs on to you and shakes your tree until you become a millionaire. And she actually records how long it took you and she keeps track of it. And she'll probably be telling you the average time it takes her to make her clients a millionaire. She's amazing. She's a dear friend. She's a superstar of the movie The Secret. She's the millionaire maker, Loral Langemeier. Loral, are you on the line? Loral, please unmute yourself.

**Loral Langemeier:**

I am here. Every small business owner has to have a mentor. A mentor is someone who's walked the path before you. So their job, I think and I've had a mentor since I was 17, that was just few years ago.

**Loral Langemeier:**

If you have the intention of becoming an entrepreneur and making money and getting wealthy then you form your corporation right now.

**Loral Langemeier:**

Instead of focusing on what you can't have in the struggle, you focus on what you can have. And so the illegal conversations I say at home is you don't say what you can't afford, you say well how can we afford it.

**Loral Langemeier:**

I mean last I checked and I always say this is kind of funny, but Christopher Columbus did not discover Americas so we could have jobs. He discovered it for entrepreneurs and for freedom and we have lost it. We lost it from, I mean generations have lost it, it is time to bring spirit back. I mean, that's where the money's made.

**Loral Langemeier:**

It's I want to be a millionaire. And I'm going to change my choices, my way of living and really get in action around creating that for myself and my life.

**Loral Langemeier:**

The traditional financial planning world doesn't work if you really want to be wealthy. The traditional financial planning world is designed that you maybe stay stable. It's designed for you to make less as you get older.

**Loral Langemeier:**

I'm Loral Langemeier the Millionaire Maker. I want you to follow me on Instagram, make sure you turn on your post notifications so you get all my messages.

**Loral Langemeier:**

What we talked about in the millionaire maker is money makeovers and how do you really recreate? Most people are focusing on debt. What we want you to focus on is creating more.

**Loral Langemeier:**

I'd say 80% of my coaching that I do one on one with folks is about their psychology and the way they think. You can run from creditors, but you can't run from your credit score.

**Loral Langemeier:**

You really have to get your money working for you. Most people don't know how to invest, they're investing poorly. They're in single digit numbers. Millionaires, don't do that.

**Loral Langemeier:**

All right, all right. How are you dear friend?

**Raymond Aaron:**

I love you. I haven't seen you since your wedding for God's sakes.

**Loral Langemeier:**

I know, how do I come live. I have my PowerPoint up here but I want to see your lovely face.

**Raymond Aaron:**

Well, I can't tell if my faces on the screen. It's one of the problems that go to webinar. But I-

**Loral Langemeier:**

So is my little face on the screen?

**Raymond Aaron:**

I can see your screen, but I think your face is not on the screen. But my Francis is working on it and just start your presentation. You are the final presentation. I've saved the best for last. Go for it Loral.

**Loral Langemeier:**

I am going to. I'm just looking on my screen. I think we're good.

**Raymond Aaron:**

Yes, I can see your screen.

**Loral Langemeier:**

And then I also am very active in chat. I've been doing these like you know from going from an offline stage. It was March 7th, that I was Houston, Texas, and that was it. Well, we start, we actually came back. We were doing a live event here in the Reno, Tahoe area when we started seeing and hearing.

**Loral Langemeier:**

One of the things which I can't wait to see you, it's been so long, but I call my go to's. So I called world leading economists, my billionaires saying what's really, obviously, there's a virus and then there's the political undercurrent, what's really going on? And they said, get the heck out of the market's going to go. March 17th, the market hit the lowest its hit since 1929. So, we'd pivoted like immediately. Actually, that day. We went live and I started a group Millionaires in Training. I said never before have me and my team been planning and training for a time like this to be worldwide and help people with money.

**Loral Langemeier:**

So I love that you're doing the summit. I appreciate being here. And those of you listening, get a pen and paper because we're going to go through a financial first aid kit. We're going to go through where do you really need to be? There is so many myths. One of the things that's happened with this COVID around the world is everybody went home, and everyone immediately became an expert. And what's interesting for a lot of you is how do you weave through what's the truth? And I'm just going to tell you, this is it. This is exactly what you need to be doing. I have recorded probably 50 to 60 hours of sequence, depending on where you are. So again, a pen and a paper, we're going to go through that. Where are you? What do you need? And how can we help you best?

**Loral Langemeier:**

So I am going to be in the chat. I will try to multitask my best. I'm not as used to this as I am Zoom but I'll figure it out. I know Francis, so you're out here private. So if everyone else can chat, I don't know if they can chat with me or Francis you can facilitate questions to me, however, we want to do that. But it's really important. Right now, never has the world been shut down, ever, ever. 1933, well 1913, the United States Federal Reserve managed by the central banks, Canada's managed by central banks. I know that people from all over the world so I'm going to speak more globally and internationally.

**Loral Langemeier:**

And by use, US vernacular, I have taught everywhere but Antarctica, it works in principle, but I'm telling you works around the world. I have clients I'm working with all over the world, and you have got to get your financial life together. And if 2008, '9 and '10 and the financial crisis wasn't bad enough, this one's different. And I'll be explaining how different, why it's different, and what you need to be doing to take care of yourself as you go into this.

**Loral Langemeier:**

So one sec I need to get some technical . . . There. Okay, sorry about that. I'm not used to your GoToWebinar, I'm used to Zoom and moving around the slides. So those of you that are out there, again, get a pen and paper, and let's walk through where you are, who you are, and what we can do to help you? So there's like three people that are happening right now in the world, right? I'd say those who live paycheck to paycheck which by the way, 47% of the world live paycheck to paycheck. 47% is the statistic. And then there's the folks who got laid off.

**Loral Langemeier:**

And again, I'm speaking a lot of times in US vernacular, and it's just as bad across the world. 24 million people unemployed, most are standing in unemployment lines, not getting checks in the socialized country. So I have a lot of clients in Australia, Canada and the UK. You have a very different system and stimulus package. You're getting a couple grand per month for four months. The question is, what are you going to do with it? Are you going to use it like a lottery ticket, or are you going to do something to change your life?

**Loral Langemeier:**

Never before in the history of our world has the world been shut down, and never in the history of our world have we been able to what I call, I'm calling this crash the indiscriminate crash because it didn't matter. Like there is no way that you can't make money in this economy. It is a world leading opportunity. So if you live paycheck to paycheck, so what? If you have been laid off, perfect. Now you have time to become an entrepreneur, you have nothing else to do besides watch Netflix Originals or whatever you're doing to as Sharon Lechter might . . . I call her my financial mom says be drifting. It is time for you to start getting your money together and deciding where you're going to invest it.

**Loral Langemeier:**

Somebody in your town owns most of the town or a variety people do. Why aren't you owning more of your town? So in each community around the world, you either create or you consume, and most people consume and expect the entrepreneur who basically gives the jobs. I mean, entrepreneurialism is the financial engine of the world. And most people are just consuming, so why not? And I know if you're listening to Raymond, you've got to be creating or at least thinking about creating. Use this time right now to tune in and listen and become a great entrepreneur.

**Loral Langemeier:**

See, we are trained so horribly. I'm going to go through how we're trained, what we need to be thinking and doing today, and what do you need to be doing very shortly. Because this isn't going to be like 2008, '9, and '10 in the slow recovery. This is going to go very quickly, the market's already recovering, right? So if you missed March 17th, 18th it's not that there aren't opportunities but you missed world class opportunities, real estate, businesses, cannabis, cryptocurrency, you name it, it is a worldwide indiscriminate time for whoever is most organized will pick up the most assets and the greatest transfer of wealth is going to happen right before our eyes.

**Loral Langemeier:**

One year from now, Raymond, I promise you, the people who pay attention and get in line and do things the way we're going to talk about doing things will be very, very wealthy if not millionaires. You said, how long does it take to be a millionaire? Well, these are my books that I wrote. So these are my three millionaire maker books. The first one Becoming A Millionaire, the promise is three to five years. So think like a university degree. Cash Machine: How To Build A Seven Figure Business While Cycle Investing, how to invest outside of Wall Street, put more cash in your pocket for all of you listening, you will be given that book just for listening today and putting more cash in your pocket is like the 21st century lemonade stand. It's for all of you that need to be making money.

**Loral Langemeier:**

And then if you don't have the yes energy, none of this is going to happen. So with that, again, if you didn't get a pen and paper, let's get out and get that done. I'm going to be skipping forward in my presentation. I hope you already watched that.

**Loral Langemeier:**

All right, so again, this is my disclaimer. I'm not a financial planner, a lawyer, a tax strategist. I've just got 25 years of some of the extraordinary experience and not only becoming a multimillionaire, teaching others how to do it. So let's get going. Here's what I teach. I teach what's called the Millionaire Matrix. And again, any of the slides or anything like that, Francis and Raymond. I know Francis you're supporting the broadcast. If anybody has questions, please either announce them out to me or they can put them in the chat if they can, and I will answer them and if they would like a copy of the presentation, they can have that towards the end just get in touch with Raymond's team.

**Francis:**

Loral, I'm going to make them an organizer so you can see the questions in the questions box.

**Loral Langemeier:**

Oh, perfect.

**Francis:**

You should be all set.

**Loral Langemeier:**

So I just go click on the little questions box?

**Francis:**

Yes.

**Loral Langemeier:**

Oh, look at all those people, awesome. What a great group.

**Francis:**

[crosstalk 00:12:59] Just so you're aware, we actually have a lot of people on YouTube and Facebook as well. So I'll relay those questions if needed.

**Loral Langemeier:**

Okay, awesome. And so all of you, I mean, ask questions. If I'm like in a thought track, I'll get to them. But I'm very used to, as my team knows of interacting with the audience and interacting with your group. And those of you that have really personal questions, if we even have time I can come live and answer them. This is one of the most important times of your life for you to pay attention.

**Loral Langemeier:**

We're not taught about money, we're not taught to be entrepreneurs. We were taught to go get a job, maximize your RSP and pension retirement, and then hope to God the whole thing works out and then not go into debt. I'm going to tell you right now that information is obsolete, absolutely obsolete. I'm going to tell you how you need to not only get going, go to where we're going and it's coming very soon.

**Loral Langemeier:**

So I'll tell you a little bit backdrop since there are so many new people that probably don't know my background. I grew up in a farm in Nebraska for those of you around the world, that's right in the center of the United States. And so I grew up on a big family farm. At 17 I was going to go off to university to become a lawyer. I met Denis Waitley, actually in Canada. And by the way, those of you who are listening and saying, "She's just an aggressive American," I'm married to a Canadian. I've been with him for over five years, Raymond was at our wedding. It was quite the celebration. And I had clients from six continents around the world in that room at our wedding.

**Loral Langemeier:**

So clients, not clients, they're friends, they're family, because this is really important, and no one has taught you money. And what you think you've learned about money is probably wrong. And I'm going to just dispel a lot of myths. So when I wrote The Millionaire Maker, I actually was a millionaire in 1999. So when I... I'll go back to my story. So when I was 17 I read Think and Grow Rich, I thought, "Oh my gosh, this is totally my conversation." Didn't grow up this conversation, didn't grow up with money, went on to university, got a finance degree, got a master's in Exercise Physiology, by 24 put those degrees together and was doing analysis of what it was costing companies to have unhealthy employees.

**Loral Langemeier:**

So I was part of the big early 90s, corporate fitness and corporate wellness revolution, wrote a book, actually back then too, and moved to New Orleans to build fitness centers on offshore rigs. I got a big contract with Chevron at 24 years old, they gave me millions of dollars on a big huge forecast and said, "This is how much money you have to spend and build fitness centers." And I said, "Absolutely."

**Loral Langemeier:**

And I want you all to think as we're having this quick conversation about your yes moments because that was a yes moment. Because when you say yes, it isn't about figuring out how to do it and I want you to write this down. It's figuring out who knows how to do it. So when you start figuring out how to put teams together, you're going to make your path to being a millionaire much quicker than those of you who haven't.

**Loral Langemeier:**

So when I became a millionaire, I was a real estate and gas and oil millionaire. So I did the homework at Chevron in 1996. I met Robert Kiyosaki, Sharon Lechter. Sharon is like I said, my financial mom, she was at our wedding in Banff, Canada as well. And it was quite the event. Hundreds and hundreds of people from around the world came. And we had so much fun. I love Canada, by the way, love skiing in Canada. We were there and I'll never forget this. I give her so much credibility to share in helping develop me and who I've become. And because in 1999, I knew I was going to be a mom.

**Loral Langemeier:**

So I was going to be mom and the father didn't want to be a dad. So I knew I was going to walk into parenting as a single mom. So my son Logan is now 20. And I that year said this is it. For some of you, you are sitting exactly on the opportunity that I had in 1999. Is I had a lot going right. So if you look at the screen there's a whole compartment of making money, there's keeping money, there's investing money and having a team. I was good at making money in a team but I really wasn't keeping it because I was skiing all over the world playing and I wasn't investing very well.

**Loral Langemeier:**

So in 1999 I said, "Oh my gosh, I'm going to be a single mom. I have nine months to really get it together." And I hired mentors way, way my senior and were really rigorous with me which is why I'm very rigorous. Like Raymond said I will shake the tree and be really, really, really straight with you about what you need to do and when and sequencing is a term that I brought to money because when you do the right thing at the right time things go faster. It's like the compounding power of money.

**Loral Langemeier:**

So right time, right thing, you start moving. So I became a millionaire in 1999, gas and oil, real estate and I started doing real estate tours around the country. At one point I had done over 1000 real estate transactions, got out of the market before the 2008 crash. 2004 I wrote my first book. Again, message to a lot of you if you have a book and you get it out because more is not coming. Meaning I have another book coming on July 4th, I'm going to be launching a *How To Make Kid Millionaire Book* because my kids have been millionaires before they were out of their teens.

**Loral Langemeier:**

I have a daughter that's 13, she is as well. I'm partnering with an Air Force fighter pilot Lieutenant who made his kids millionaires in Germany very different way. We're co-authoring a book. And my point is if you ever believe in the true law of attraction, I mean, you all have amazing content, but you're not getting it out of your head. So I like very quickly did a book with Jay Conrad Levinson, put it out. I look back at now, it's called Gorilla Wealth and I look back, I look, "Oh my gosh, it was so green. I was so . . . " I shouldn't say immature, but I mean, boy, I didn't know what I know now. But my point is I got it out.

**Loral Langemeier:**

Three weeks later, three months later, and it's like a very short period of time McGraw Hill comes to me and said, "Will you write a three book series called *The Millionaire Maker*?" I said, "No, I don't know how to write. I can talk. I'm great at talking. We can record me, somebody's got to edit, somebody's got to . . . " So I got a ghostwriter. So they would edit my language and I would go, go, go. And that's how I write books, it's very, very quick. I do them very quick. I talk them, transcribe them, move very quickly.

**Loral Langemeier:**

I did a New York Times bestseller in 2006, '7, '8. I did 2009, Put More Cash In Your Pocket, which was a recovery to the economy. And then in 2012, I wanted to be a Hay House author, with that group, and Wayne Dyer and that group. So I did Yes Energy book, because you got to have yes energy and you've got to have persistence.

**Loral Langemeier:**

So all of that I took together and I said, "Well, how do you become a millionaire, really? And I've just perfected it. And this isn't what I've done. I studied millionaires, I studied the Rockefeller family, the Roosevelt family, the seven families who went to Jekyll Island. I have studied and said, "How do people become millionaires?" And this is what we came up with. It's a very simple way of teaching how to become a millionaire. Start with make money.

**Loral Langemeier:**

So first of all, it's in an infinity loop because for all of you, the minute you walk on the planet, the minute you walk off, you will deal with money every day. Now most of you do it completely unconsciously and benign, and you have no idea, right? And you run your financial life by the balance in your checkbook, which is completely irresponsible. You don't look at your checkbook, you look at your P&L.

**Loral Langemeier:**

So you look at a P&L, you look at a balance sheet, you look at a proforma, you look at cash flow, which means you got to bet on yourself as an entrepreneur. See, but we're not taught that, we're taught to make money you have a job. So that's not how wealthy people have lived. So we're teaching you how to act think and make money the way the wealthy do. So inside the make money category, and we go into deep, deep training over four years, you're going to learn this. Now here's what I know about becoming a millionaire, why I'm frontline teaching every day. I broadcast every day, every day, every day, because I have millionaires in training and I'm helping you become a millionaire in training.

**Loral Langemeier:**

If you're already a multi millionaire, then let's go to multi fast, fast because there's opportunities everywhere if you know how to look for them. And that's the step I really like to teach is how do you, once you have some money, where are you putting it? And if you missed the market should you say and I can't tell you we'd have to have a private conversation about that. But do you need to make money right now? Absolutely. Because the total fallout's not done.

**Loral Langemeier:**

When people sit home for this long and decide if they're a, going back to work, my aggressive goal for all of you is if you're not a good entrepreneur, let's spend time. I can't wait to make you a great entrepreneur. I do a very cool workshop that I'm going to invite you all to, and we just did one last week. It's Wednesday night to Friday night. It's literally a 48 hour Blitz, and you will make money. So I have people literally in 48 hours making 2100, 3800. I think the winner was right about $4100 by the time the whole of that was over. I had people make hundreds of dollars like everybody's making money. I think one of the lowest one was $9 for their offer.

**Loral Langemeier:**

So we're going to teach you how to put that revenue funnel together, how to do it. I'm going to go into the details of how to do this. But I don't care how much money you have or what your net worth is? Knowing how to make money in any time, any economic time and then knowing what to do with your money is some of the most critical skills I think you could learn. And I think about it, and Raymond, you and I are just such mentor advocates. So many of you, you paid for weight loss programs, you've paid for beauty age, you've paid for gyms, you've paid for music lessons, you've paid to go on elaborate vacations, you probably have a vehicle that's sitting out in your driveway, that's more than any tuition you've ever paid for any financial education.

**Loral Langemeier:**

So this time, is your time without any interruption to stop and learn and learn how do you make money? How do you keep money? How do you invest it and how you use a team. So with that, we're going to forward to the next slide and here's how we're taught. So I'm going to go back a little bit to history. I'm going to teach you a little history lesson. So those of you again that have a pen and paper or you want to screenshot any of this, you are welcome to do it. And Francis at anytime feed me questions. So I can be very relevant to our group that's out there.

**Loral Langemeier:**

So here's what we're taught. This has been since 1933. Prior to 1933, all of our ancestors were entrepreneurs. And then Jekyll Island and the industrial age happened, and the war happened, and notice this is very US lead. And what's interesting is, this is what we're taught. And I put this in a lot of Canadian vernacular. So it's kind of both ways. It's very similar to Australia as well as the UK. I've taught a lot in South Africa, Raymond and I have been there together. And those of you that don't think you need to pay attention to this, I can tell you every world economist that I've had on my broadcasts and is guiding and validating what I'm telling you is exactly what's going to happen and like you need to pay attention. Is Australia and Canada are going to see a recession that they have not seen probably in your lifetime.

**Loral Langemeier:**

Australia is going to get hit very, very hard. The real estate is going to need an enormous reset. Vancouver's going to get hit. Toronto is going to have a little bit of a correction. Calgary has been on the ground since 2017 when the oil prices dropped and doesn't have a new way to get back up. So, if you are in those countries you need to pay attention to what you're . . . And we're in the life, not in the future of, in the life of digital currency. Canada's looking at it, US is looking at it and it's not because of COVID. Like there's a piece of come on, folks. Yes, there's a virus. Yes, it's dangerous. Yes, people are dying. Yes, it's critical. And there is an entire financial infrastructure that is going on beneath you while you either sit home on vacation with your head in the sand and drip as Sharon says, or you are pulling your head up and saying this time, this is my time.

**Loral Langemeier:**

I want you to be so motivated and so excited. Even if you don't know what you're doing. Know that you can have the greatest transfer of wealth and it can happen anywhere in the world. Like I want you to think how can I come out of this and be something different? Your time to co-create and create yourself new and different is right at your fingertips.

**Loral Langemeier:**

So let's dig in. As an employee, your average salary if you make 100 and again, this is part of the . . . This is online, some of the statistics are a little varied, but we pulled it offline and we wanted . . . In America is $89,000. Just so, you know, the variance of socialized countries, the Canadian countries, Australian countries, UK paid much higher salaries, but you also get much higher tax.

**Loral Langemeier:**

So if you make 169 though, my point is you are in the upper 25% of those who make the most money in Canada. US it's 89,000 and I have to look at the statistics across the rest of the world. But here's the principle of it. You make money, you get taxed. That's a government mandate. Anywhere in the world, this is true. And then you're offered to put money away. In America it's called the 401k, in Canada is an RSP. If you want and you're a little more independent, you can do a TFSA and Australia it's called the superannuation.

**Loral Langemeier:**

And then because you're such good people, you made money, you paid your taxes, you put money away, and do you understand who's investing your RSP money? It's going in one place, it's going into the stock market, into bonds and mutual funds. You don't get to self direct, you don't get to say I want to go buy real estate, you've got to use that with a little bit of cash, you have leftover. But if you were really good, you could go on vacation, you're going to go on a holiday, whoa. Then you're taught that debt and credit cards are bad, and that's totally not true.

**Loral Langemeier:**

Using proper debt structures, has created more wealth in the world than any other mechanism. And I'm going to say it again, debt, specific debt has created more wealth, for more wealthy people than any other vehicle. And most people have no idea how to use debt because you're taught that debt's bad. It's not bad, it's a tool for wealth and I'm going to teach you that in a moment.

**Loral Langemeier:**

Then you're taught to retire. So there's the interesting thing about retirement. It's not even a financial word. It's an agricultural word that means to put cattle to pasture today. So what an awesome goal, let's go work forever, get taxed to pieces, put money away that you can't control, maybe go on two or three weeks, because that's all you have deserved or work for or somebody else told you that's all you get. Keep debt and credit cards to a minimum and not use them, and then go retire so you can die. Like who wants this? And then you file taxes on a very fixed date.

**Loral Langemeier:**

Now, that's what we're taught, it's a worldwide thing. That's what we call the sheep mentality, follow along and behave. And I'm not saying anything is illegal or not behaving, but

I'm just signing out, people get rich. Here you go. You make money inside companies. So here's the easiest way I teach it. Companies make money, individuals get taxed. That's it, right? As an individual you don't get to write off your car, as an individual you don't get to write off any, you know, if you want to do a book with Raymond or you want to do some mentoring or coaching with me, you can't write that off as a business deduction because you don't have a business, right?

**Loral Langemeier:**

So you make money and you get taxed, but as a company, you're making money and then you get depreciation. That's the Canadian version, America's got 81,000 pages of tax code, which is superior worldwide. The US corporate structures are, they are superior. I mean, I've had companies in different countries, a variety of places in the world and there's no GST in America, you make it, you spend it, and then you put more away. In America it's called the solo 401k. There's, again, in principle, I don't want to get to the little micro details. I want you to see the principle of the money. Kiyosaki had wrote it out in his book really well, you can make it, get taxed and spend what's left, or you can make it, spend the legal deductions and then pay tax. So this is about your pattern of money is what I want you seeing and how wealthy people do it.

**Loral Langemeier:**

Companies make money, you get deductions, you don't go on vacations, you go on business trips, like I have real estate, a lot of real estate. I'm in the wine business. So I can travel anywhere. I can go to Canada, I can go to South Africa, I can go to Australia, and very strict tax rules, but I can actually write off a business trip by looking at real estate, looking at wine, I can speak,

I can sell my books in different countries. I go on business trips, right? You take your . . . You don't go on vacations.

**Loral Langemeier:**

I remember my son, and Raymond you know Logan really well. I remember him coming home from his kindergarten, his first year in school. And we had just gotten back from Hawaii. And he comes home and he puts his little hands on his hips. He's so irritated. He's like, "Oh, mum, everybody teased me today." They said, "Where did you go on vacation?" And he said, "I didn't even know what that word was." He said, "I told them I went on a business trip, and they didn't understand." So I'm just telling you, folks, it's like, it's a different way of life when you raise your kids this way. I can't wait to teach you guys.

**Loral Langemeier:**

If this has been interesting to you, let me have your kids. Because your kids need to know and they're in such a different world. Half of the jobs aren't even made up. We're so high tech. We're so different. I mean, hacking's a career right now, gaming is a career right now. And some of your parents like you got to like get current to how to live corporate life and how to use debt. Debt and credit cards are fabulous. When you can get debt or credit cards at zero, two, three, to 5% and you can invest at 10, 12, 15, 20, 30 why would you ever pay off really cheap debt just to say you are debt free?

**Loral Langemeier:**

Very wealthy families will carry debt for generations. Think about a house or a shopping mall. And I'm not saying it's not okay to pay off real estate at some point like, so don't hear that it's, you know, for some families, it's your rules. I'm just saying there are strategies to have this be very different. And debt in this environment right now will pick up more wealth than anything you have ever seen. And I'll give you some examples about that. You don't retire when you're wealthy, you have a Freedom Day. You create your life the way you want, and you file throughout the year with tax strategies.

**Loral Langemeier:**

So here's the challenge, 1933 that left side is how we were taught. But the wealthy have always lived on the right side, and I'm going to continue to refer to are you living on the right side? On my presentation. So take a little screenshot of this in your mind or yourself and say, "Am I living on the right side? Do I have a company? Am I doing the right taxes? Am I doing things to the maximum of my family benefit?" This isn't about teaching you any weird, or even esoteric, or conspiracy stuff. This is how people live. Your company makes money, you get the tax benefits because you're an employee and you're actually stimulating the economy, you're providing amazing valuable services to people and changing their life. You take business trips, you use that differently. And I can tell you folks right now, there's a third column coming to the far right. And that is digital and cryptocurrency. And it is very, very real in the world and it's very active in the world.

**Loral Langemeier:**

I know people have bought real estate with digital currency. I know people who have bought cars, who transact for groceries. Some of you are so far away from that conversation. You don't even understand it. I'm going to be doing a very deep dive with some of the world's leading billionaires. Jim Blasco, Mike [inaudible 00:32:15]. They're just guys and a lot of them live in Puerto Rico are billionaires in crypto or in projects that I'm very,

very familiar with. And we're going to be helping you learn because you're going to have to learn.

**Loral Langemeier:**

I think, again, to say that handling cash has germs, it's had germs for decades. I mean, come on, folks, you know that. So what's it really about? It's not the digital currencies just come because I don't want to touch gas, because COVID it's been in the works. Here in the United States there's financial Institute's that told everybody don't invest, don't invest, don't invest in cryptocurrency, and then they were the very first financial Institute to come out with a cryptocurrency.

**Loral Langemeier:**

So what you're being told and what actually happens, just be in the know, be in the know. I can't even get into that whole like infrastructure conversation, there is a financial infrastructure that's beneath you, and my question to you, is your own family's financial infrastructure ready for what's in front of you? And right now, I literally want you to look up, I want you to look around your community and say, "Are those restaurants going to come back?" And you say, "I don't know. I'm going to give you the script. I can give you the script for that."

**Loral Langemeier:**

There's a car dealership, in a very large town, a client of mine called and said, "Hey, this car dealership's going south, and how can we pick it up?" And I said, "We'll see if they'll do an owner carry back." So that's a debt structure. I said we could put in a little bit of money which we could borrow the money, right? Use other people's money, go into credit, and basically there are ways where you have to put no money in. See the biggest lie, so I'm going to keep expelling lies. Number one, if you don't make decisions by your financial checkbook. Number two, you don't have to have money to make money. I'm going to teach you in my marketplace, I teach a marketplace place technology. You can make money out of nothing. You can make money by putting deals together. Like I can go, I am, we're borrowing money and then we're going to take that money and we're going to do an owner carry back to another which is using their credit. And in between, we're going to own a car dealership.

**Loral Langemeier:**

And I say we because I'm actually probably going to help do this one. I usually don't ever do that, but it's kind of fun to say you're a car dealership. There are subway franchises going south in the United States. There are Chick-Fil-A's, McDonald's, there are so many businesses that are not going to make it. There are restaurants that aren't going to make it, that are like even higher end restaurants, there are hair salons, there's chiropractic businesses.

**Loral Langemeier:**

I mean, right now most of my work that I'm doing with people, and Francis, I'm looking down I don't see a lot of questions in here.

**Francis:**

Not too many questions.

**Loral Langemeier:**

Not very many questions, everybody's just like at the edge of their seat. Ask me some questions. So think about like my favorite thing to do right now is to help you strategize your business, get really creative with you about how can you take the revenue streams you had pre-COVID and when you had to go home, how do you now make a lot of money doing it? And there are so many ways, for so many of you to pick up and some of you, you don't want to make a big business right now, but maybe just at least pick a couple extra thousand dollars.

**Loral Langemeier:**

Some of you need to make $5,000, some of you need to make $10,000, some of you need to learn how to see what's in your community, like auto body shops, are they going to make it or not? I don't know, I'm going to give you a script in a little moment. Like, don't be the people that just sit home and say 2020 went by, because it's going to be a year from now. It's, I'm not going to say there's always opportunities, but do three and four, right? The third quarter and the fourth quarter of this year is when you're going to see businesses completely fall down and be on big sales. You're going to see more and more real estate fall completely down when this comes back up.

**Loral Langemeier:**

People, they're learning they can live a little different. So take responsibility for how you want to do it. Like design your life right now. It's such a good opportunity. Let's get into some real tactics really quick. So that's the big frame. The big frame is my goal is to work with you, to strategize with you, to live on the left side. I mean, I'll live on the right side, live that corporate life, understand it, whatever country you're from, and then truly move even more into what's going to become very digital as a transactional space around the world.

**Loral Langemeier:**

And I just want to give you one clue, because I'm probably not going to go back to a lot of digital and crypto. But you have to think right now the US and Canadian dollar, I know very well, because my husband's Canadian. The exchange is not good for you guys, right up in Canada. Great for us. So you can imagine though, that we have the same currency, right? We have the same currency, we could exchange through a wallet. I could just pay you in that digital currency and there's no exchange rate, there's no exchange fees, there's no transfer fees, there's no bank fees, there's no wiring fees, all of it changes. This is going to be life changing. So some of you who don't have your basics organized, think where we're going, think where we're going if you aren't ready.

**Loral Langemeier:**

So what do you do today? Like, what do you do now? So what you needed to have done now is stop the bleeding. So what do you do? Well, you're going to, I have a very spaced approach to your bad debt, your lifestyle, where you've just been overspending and things that aren't having any ROI. And so you've got to stop the bleeding. So that means really look at what you're spending, do you need it now? Has it really served your life in a way that's enhanced your life, or is it just been what you need? Can you call your credit card companies and delay or defer payments? Absolutely. There's a whole structure I'm going to go into like around what you can do for that.

**Loral Langemeier:**

Mortgages, typically, I would say do not delay your mortgages, because that's going to affect your credit. Again, that's a worldwide principle. If you are a landlord, talk to your tenant. If you're a tenant, talk to your landlords. I mean, three of the biggest C's I'm talking about is collaborate, get really creative, and find the cash and talk about cash with each other very quickly. Sorry, I have a typo right there. I just noticed that, pivot to some new money meaning, let me teach you how to make some new money. Think about what could you do now? And it's not Loral I don't know how to go online, then hire somebody, partner with somebody, you can collaborate, be creative about what you can do.

**Loral Langemeier:**

I've had some most creative ideas of like in some restaurants. I'll give you some ideas. So like some restaurants and towns that have different kinds of chefs, like why have three or two restaurants with the entire kitchen staff and even opening up the inventories, why not collaborate and have two or three chefs that provide different foods all come and collaborate into one kitchen, one cost versus three costs. And so collaborate, get creative, generate different menus, generate different things and come up with a delivery service.

**Loral Langemeier:**

The other thing, a big piece that I'm going to say not only restaurants but cleaning, I mean, a lot of the food chains got stopped, right? And I'm going to say the supply chains better like the actual accurate word. The supply chains got stopped. I live in northern Nevada, like Tahoe, Nevada area. And there were trucks on their way to all the casinos that are here also in Las Vegas. And where did all of that supply chain go? There were restaurants, there were small mom and pop kind of grocery stores. There were chiropractors that actually took some of the supplies where they're partnered with supplies became more of a marketplace.

**Loral Langemeier:**

You have to think there are so many ways. Think of the kids that are all home and do not tell me that teachers know how to teach online. So if you are a better teacher online, why aren't you helping the teachers not for free, but helping them get the education and the information. One of the systemic problems we're going to have across the world is when all of the kids do go back to school after missing three, four potentially five months, what is that going to look like in the education system and the year, half a year that they've just missed? And don't underestimate the problematic and systematic damage that's going to do financially to a lot of people.

**Loral Langemeier:**

And then I want you to position for new growth. Again, opportunities are everywhere. If you could think about the companies around your town, and what are the two or three things you'd like to own? That's where I want you thinking, right? How do you own it? And here's how simple some of those scripts are. I promise you I'd give you a little bit of a script. If you're going to walk into say a mom and pop auto body shop or say there's a [serious 00:40:41] shop that's next door down the street, there's a restaurant, there's a hair supply store, they may not. So number one, inventories have expired potentially. So you have to think well that's going to be a financial problem when they actually open up their doors. Is any of the inventory even okay anymore? Is there expiration on it? Do they really want to hire people back?

**Loral Langemeier:**

And people are going to need, the business owners are going to need cash. So if you've been one of those employees, and you've been stockpiling cash, you say, "Well, how do I walk in and how do I own part of their company?" And here's the interesting news about it. It's probably not for sale, right? So then you say, here's my advice to you, always get into a financial conversation. So how has it been for you would be my script? And believe me, I'm using it. How's it been for you? And they'll say their parts. And I'll say, "No, not financially. How has it been and how do you believe that you're going to live through this? And are you going to open up again? And they'll look at you a little odd, especially if you are in a more what I call conservative states and conversations.

**Loral Langemeier:**

And you're going to say to them, I can help because I'm going to help you. You're going to bring these ideas and opportunities back and I'm going to coach you through how to do some of these things. And some of the options, you could be the business loan. You could be the loan. You could say you know what, for 20 grand, for 30 grand, what do you need? And there's an analysis, I can help you do an analysis. What do you need to get back on your feet if you do want to open your doors again?

**Loral Langemeier:**

And you be the business loan and say, "Well," if say they need $50,000, and you happen to have it, say, "For 50,000, I could either do a loan at 10 or 12%, or whatever, we can negotiate, maybe eight or nine that's kind of low, or you know what, for $450,000 welcome to Dragon's Den and Shark Tanks folks, I'll actually be a partner." Now, the percent depends on their financials. And again, there's formulas around how to do this, but I am telling you, you are in the greatest transfer of wealth.

**Loral Langemeier:**

So what that means, this is what I mean by transfer of wealth is something needs to come back into the economy to create more cash and to create more movement, create more jobs, and it's not going to be able to because it's too short in capital, you could be the capital partner, you could be that first acquisition on like they do on Dragon's Den and Shark Tank. And what I think the difference that a lot of you have to hear this from is I'm not talking about new stuff. I'm talking about stuff that's been around for a long time, right? The supply, the hobby shop, right? The art supplies. I mean, you got to think, the paint stores.

**Loral Langemeier:**

If you think about all the supplies that have been stuck, why can't you own part of it? And I want you to start thinking, I could do this. And you say, "Well, what if I only have 10,000?" Well, I bet you know four people that have 10,000 and together you've got 50,000 and now you can do it. And I'm using that as an example but I want you thinking, I want you so motivated to say I'm going to go figure out how to make money, and then I'm going to go look in my community and say what am I going to buy? And some of you by the way, are really high in community.

**Loral Langemeier:**

So, one of my greatest motto's is live where you want and invest where it makes sense. Like I live in Lake Tahoe, Nevada area, I live at the lake. I mean, world class and where I like to go is always beautiful places. That doesn't mean I invest my rental real estates there. My rental real estate is in Kansas, Missouri, Ohio, right?

**Loral Langemeier:**

I mean, invest where it makes a lot of cash flow sense. And if you don't know how to find those areas, one of the bonuses I'm going to give all of you who continue to move forward with us, is we're going to give you a real estate tour. And that's not the big fancy bus ones. I mean, you're going to watch houses be built, you're going to see how rentals are listed. Like we're real. I want you to really get like I could do this. So many of you have been so ill prepared and ill trained and you think TV, and all those TV shows are your education, it's not. TV's is entertainment. Believe me. I know I used to be Dr. Phil's expert. It was in 2008, '9 and '10. It was in those really, really down markets when I became this expert. He said, Loral we got to help the nation. I'm going to find families that are going to apply for money makeover. I'm going to send you to that, that town, and you're going to go make them over. I'm like, "All right."

**Loral Langemeier:**

And so we did and I can tell you, some people really want to have a different life, and some people don't. Some people are just used to being in pain. And I can't imagine, in this time, when you and your family have the opportunity to bring a family conversation and say, let's be business owners, and so many of you probably say, "I don't know how to be." I know you don't know how to be, but I know how to be. I've got thousands of clients that know how to be. So I don't know, you're going to find a team, you're going to find a partnership, you just have to raise your hand and say, "I'm going to learn this stuff." I'm going to learn it for the first time in my life, and I'm going to go on a real estate tour with Loral and her team, and I'm going to figure out how to do it, and I'm going to figure out how to look at businesses, and I'm going to own something different.

**Loral Langemeier:**

I want you to make a big wish list. And do you get in and out of the market? I don't know. Oh, I also have another gift for you. I have a software that I'm going to give all of you. It's a free software. And we've been using it for years. So because of the software, it's algorithmically programmed to take you out of the market before the market falls. So I only lost 2.8% in my market. Anybody in the software only lost about two to 3%.

**Loral Langemeier:**

I think one person might have lost eight or nine because they were in a really aggressive, they were trading by themselves outside of the software. My point is, there are things that the wealthy do, that people do, to just, again, think and act and behave differently.

**Loral Langemeier:**

So as you look at business options, what can you do? Well, you could be a business owner, or you could get a business, you can defer payments, you could protect your credit at all costs, protect your credit, I'm probably one of the only financial education gurus that teaches you that your credit is pristine. So now let's just say you blew your credit already, and you don't have good credit, well, then you're going to partner to somebody who has good credit, right?

**Loral Langemeier:**

And if you have you run out of credit, because you bought too much stuff, like I have a lot of real estate investors where they bought their 10th, 11th or 12th home and they just don't have any credit left. Well then that's when you take on a partner and you use their credit. There are so many creative ways that I can't wait to continue. Right now it's just kind of a smorgasbord. I wanted to give you this amazing smorgasbord of what you can do because it's available.

**Loral Langemeier:**

Now, one of the things we're going to do as we work together is we're going to design a business model. This has been my business model for years. So there's a lot of marketing, we'll teach you about. And then again, books, webinars, previews is what I've been doing, whether it was a real estate tour to I did a three days to cash for a long time. Now I'm online, it's called the virtual marketplace. And that's now our workshop. I still hopefully in July, we're going to be going back out to Las Vegas and doing a workshop. And I have a big table, mentoring program, and some coaching.

**Loral Langemeier:**

My point is that all of you need to look at your business models. Like don't stop creating cash at all costs. You want to really refocus your funnel. So like for us, we refocused our funnel online. We got sponsors online. We got affiliates and alliances that are all online faster than we ever did. We revamped every store in every place, I'm also moving all my work into a variety of different languages. So really, really quickly shifting your model, strategically look at your costs. I mean, I'm talking if you have no idea how to do this, I am masterful. I mean, 2008, '9 and '10 I don't know how many companies I helped save, by really, really cutting costs. And the one cut that I think too many companies are making is your human capital.

**Loral Langemeier:**

So like I right size some of my human capital, and I can explain how to do that. I had a few people self select that they didn't want to continue. But I'll tell you, we maintained almost like I'd say, 90% of our human capital. Too many companies just kind of let it go and you got to be kidding. Now you're going to work alone? Like that's suffering. And one of the biggest things all of you need to do and very quickly as modify and adjust your offers.

**Loral Langemeier:**

Change your payment structure, change your contract structure, secure deposit, pre sell, like we already started pre selling our July financial *How To Make A Millionaire Kid book*. We're already pre selling it. And so it's not coming out till July 4th. So there's so many ways to help you make money and take different payment structures. That's probably one of the most masterful things you could do in this economy. And it not only helps you but it helps other people.

**Loral Langemeier:**

One of the things I've taught some restaurants to do is if you spend $150 today, for example, you'll have $150 credit in the future once we open back up, right? So it's a way to preserve cash, one restaurant did that on that idea. And they brought in $30,000 in 24 hours. Now, they're going to have to pay that out in food later, but they didn't need the money later, which we'll deal with that if they do, they needed it today. And they were way off on the revenues and they need it today.

**Loral Langemeier:**

So if again, if you guys have questions, I would love any questions about hey, I'm in this business and I do this and I would love an idea because I love talking to all of you. And this is a handout we'll give all of you of how to build your funnel, and how to build your pricing, and how to build what you're building so you can have offers that are relevant and serving your community. And if you don't have a community, you need to get one.

**Loral Langemeier:**

Now, selling versus serving. I teach a very specific sales process in our marketplace that teaches you to do less of this, self driven, talking at you, attempting control, you deciding for people, experiencing rejection, not having congruency, right? Totally doesn't work when you are doing these techniques. Here's what you want. You don't want to close deals, you want to open relationships, you want customer driven conversations, you want to talk with people, you want to provide leadership, right?

**Loral Langemeier:**

My goal today is to provide you leadership in your financial and your money conversations. Who's helping you? How do you go all by yourself and talk to your family or your friends who are all uneducated? You don't talk to them. If your CPA and lawyer are not doing deals, why are you talking to them? They're going to say you're crazy, right? The CPAs and lawyers and financial strategists that are on our team, they do deals, they're very involved, they're millionaires.

**Loral Langemeier:**

Like you want that kind of a team who can be with you in creativity, then just telling you no, no, no. I want my client to decide what they want. You can't decide for them. You do not reject, if you told me no, today, I'd say, "Well, it's probably not now because at some point, you're going to need money." So there's just a different way to continue to serve like I am passionate about having you get your money education, because then I get a smarter conversation with you.

**Loral Langemeier:**

> Your congruence, I think you probably know from my voice, I
> mean, Raymond wouldn't have me on, I'm so congruent about
> this conversation. I live and breathe everything that I'm telling
> you, and it's about abundance for all because I love the team,
> I love helping people become millionaires, and helping the
> relationship that you get to thrive to, you totally get to thrive.

**Loral Langemeier:**

> So in my marketplace technology, which is kind of what I'm
> known for, is an ability within three to five minutes, maybe 10 if
> you're slow, you can make money. So literally, you're going to
> speak, we're going to come up with an offer, you're going to
> create a cool technology. There are all sorts of platforms we use
> when we're doing it, and literally in 48 hours . . . I know Sandy's
> out there, a few of my clients are out there. I don't know if they
> can actually talk or say anything. I was just saying, why don't
> you give a shout out, you were just there and you just everyone
> made money.

**Loral Langemeier:**

> There's a lot of people from Toronto because I've taken a couple
> tours through November and February, through Toronto. I had
> tons and tons of Canadians on selling from books to workshops
> to all sorts of fun stuff. When it comes to again making money
> and keeping money, you have to at some point, learn to invest
> it and this is money rules. So have some rules to abide by when
> it comes to your money and we will create them together in
> a conversation but what is your purpose of why you would
> invest? Is it permanent wealth or cash flow? What is your ROI?
> Return On Investment, Return Of Liability.

**Loral Langemeier:**

I should put up another one ROR like return on your relationship metrics. And then how do you measure your wealth? It's not a number. For some people for the days you can work without trading time. In this environment, you're going to trade time. Influencers trade time. There's a lot of rules that are changing around what money is and how it is. What most of you and I could almost attest to over 50% don't know how to do is have your money purely work for you. Purely work for you. Put it to work, and it doubles.

**Loral Langemeier:**

So what's the amount of time? Is it three years, is it five years? So if you had, say $300 or $300,000 in your RSP, or a pension, or somewhere, how fast could you make 300, 600 and then 601.2, and then 1.2, 2.4, right? There's a rule 72 that says normally on average, people can turn their money and double it about every seven years. Well, what if you got a little more strategic? What If you have more information? What if you have more skills and experience on your team? And notice I'm not asking you to put it on all the time.

**Loral Langemeier:**

I've got 25 plus years of teaching people how to do this. So you put me on your team, you put my CPA who's got 30 years, you put my lawyers on your team, we're hundreds and hundreds of years of experience. So what's that worth? What's that worth? I can tell you, I became a millionaire by having mentors. I've had mentors since I was 17 years old. That was just a few years ago, as you heard in my video. The greatest transfer of wealth is happening right now, and are you set up to participate? Are you going to watch this one go by or are you going to be a part of it? Our invitation is that you'd be a part of it. And let's put some band aids on where you're bleeding. Let's get that first aid kit out and really, really help you.

**Loral Langemeier:**

So we're going to do this, right? And, if you want to jump in with any questions as we go through, but let me tell you what we're going to do. I'm doing this-

**Francis:**

[crosstalk 00:55:00] questions for you if you want them now.

**Loral Langemeier:**

Yeah, let's go. Let's take some.

**Francis:**

So I'm going to group a few of these questions because they have been coming in. So a number of the questions are how do I start with little money or ground zero or not so great credit?

**Loral Langemeier:**

Okay, perfect. I love that question. Go, so first of all, you don't have to have any money to make money. And as I put the first thing that you're going to all be doing with me. You're going to have two tickets to our virtual meetup marketplace, you're gonna learn to make money. So if you don't have a lot, conserve what you have. And I have, in fact, I'm going to give it to you with all of this.

**Loral Langemeier:**

I'm going to give you like, really how do you conserve what you have and fix what you have. Some of you have little bleeding tentacles out of your financial life and you're not clear about what they are. And a lot of times it's inside how your credit card and your bank structure, especially if you're Canadian, you've got five banks to choose from. You've got all sorts of different things that you need to navigate. But clearly, I want you navigating. And if you don't have a lot of credit, you're going to partner. So partner is kind of the overarching answer, but for those of you who don't have a lot, let's become an entrepreneur and make it.

**Loral Langemeier:**

Now, I know when I say that, I'm going to teach you how to make it. The next online event we are doing is in May 13, 14, 15. That means Wednesday night at 5:00 to Friday night at 5:00, we are going to go. There will be 10 hours of content and the rest is all interaction and marketplace and you making money, reporting back into us for coaching and support.

**Loral Langemeier:**

It's very different than you've experienced anything. Because you're very active, you're going to be going from this platform to that platform, you might go to Instagram, you might go to Skype, you may come back, like it's very interactive, cool little process that I've done to teach you how to make money. If you can't do May then do June but why would you wait. If you don't have a lot you got to get started making money.

**Francis:**

Another question, again I'm grouping because I'm looking at multiple platforms here. I have my kids where do I start with them? I really want them to learn this.

**Loral Langemeier:**

Bring them with them to the marketplace. Anyone, I mean, kids are pretty switched on. I mean, I had kids on our last one. We just did our first virtual. I've been doing this work for decades, I made it up for decades. But your kids eight and older can attend. And when you get that put more cash in your pocket book because you're all going to get that. There's 1000 different ideas on how to make money. So you have to think about your kids ability to be online, to support, to do videos, there's so many things that kids can just do to be involved.

**Loral Langemeier:**

They can make jewelry, they can make food, they can . . . I mean, they can tutor other kids, my kids tutor other kids, which is a huge need right now. And by the way, a lot of kids tutoring other kids is how a lot of kids are getting through school. So should that be for free, or is that actually a business? So a lot of ideas, I got lots of kids ideas.

**Loral Langemeier:**

And the other thing too is when your kids set up a bank account as an adult, you're going to have to obviously have your name on everything but set up bank accounts for your kids when they're 12, 13. I have a complete process to teach you when your kids should have credit cards, when they should get credit. When my son was 18, he got his own corporation. And I think anywhere in the world when you're an adult, you should get your own company, you and then learn how to be an entrepreneur. Even if you go get a job. Learn how to be an entrepreneur so you can live that right side life that we're talking about. Great question.

**Francis:**

I love that answer. I have four kids myself. I'm going to group a couple more and we'll do a couple more here. What are the best opportunities right now? Is it currency? Is it gold and silver, stocks, real estate? What's the best player?

**Loral Langemeier:**

Well, that's what I mean by indiscriminate. I think they're all great. So I think the markets made its run, it dipped heavily. I think there's still things in the market. So again, I can't give you advice for things that are always still good and still low is gas and oil. There are some crypto's, crypto has really been leveled, the playing field has been leveled. I think there's some really good crypto's to get.

**Loral Langemeier:**

Everyone's got their thing about gold and silver. It's non-transactable. But should you have some, probably some but again, if you had to look at your whole portfolio and you need transactable cash gold isn't going to give it to you necessarily, unless you are in the stock market. I'm talking about physical gold. Real estate in certain markets, absolutely. I think there's real estate deals everywhere all the time. I think land is going to be great, RV parks are great, storage units are great, parking lots are great.

**Loral Langemeier:**

And then the one that I'm probably most excited about because this never happened, where you're going to have so many opportunities is businesses. I mean, businesses are going, they were all shut down. They weren't all shut down, but majority shut down. If you have any idea or want to go buy a company or partner into a company, it's a goldmine right now.

**Loral Langemeier:**

Everywhere in the world you can go buy and so why would I buy by a brick and mortar? Because they need money. They've had revenue before. There's a way to do due diligence very quickly looking at their cash flow, their customer base, their monetization, and very quickly, I mean, I have like a quick handful of things that I look at, to see if the business is even viable, and if I want to look or I move on.

**Loral Langemeier:**

So I think that that's what I mean by indiscriminate. In '8, '9 and '10 it was real estate, right? You had a huge issue and you could pick up a lot at the end of it. This one's going to be quick, it's going to be in and out. The economy coming into this was thriving, it's not going to take a lot to bring it back, but on its down moments, which is why I'm talking everyday to people, on its down moments we will in our millionaires and training groups say go, it's time, go look for the businesses that are down, go look for the real estate that's down. Private capital, I think is one of your biggest opportunities.

**Francis:**

I love that, great answer. One more question, but before I do, Dominic Mills on the Facebook feed says yes, we made money with Loral, get in touch and we'll tell you more. So got some fans of yours here in the watching other feeds online as well. Loral, so grouping this question partnering, what if I don't have skills, how do I find that partner?

**Loral Langemeier:**

Well, part of being in our marketplace, you're going to meet. Like we had 140 active people playing, making money, right? They were more in on watching but not being active. So I would say join our community, jump in, and I'm a good matchmaker, right? I'm a great matchmaker of different skills. What you don't want in a partner is somebody who has the same skill set as you, right?

**Loral Langemeier:**

What you don't want is two people bringing money but nothing else. When you think about a deal, write this down. When you think about a deal, what makes up a deal? You got to have money. Somebody's got to have money, right? There's got to be some money. There's got to be some credit, potentially, there's got to be experience, and there has got to be access to other wisdom and experience, which is kind of hard to explain, but like you can't, like I get access to a lot of deals. People offer me, "Well, I'll give you 10% if you just help me." Because you can't buy my brains. Like I have so much experience, I wouldn't even know how to take it out, and bottle it and give it to you.

**Loral Langemeier:**

And that's what you see on Shark Tank, that is what you see on Dragon's Den, is you want somebody on your team. You do not want to like two of you holding hands going out together and saying let's go buy a business, because we heard Loral. That's dangerous, right? You don't know enough. So you want to partner with really proven experienced, access, money and credit.

**Francis:**

Outstanding. Wonderful. I'll pass it back to you.

**Loral Langemeier:**

All right, cool. So here's what you're going to get. And when Raymond and I were planning this because team, I text him a whole bunch of ideas. And he said, "Do the financial first aid kit." So I said, "All right, well, I got to put together a whole bunch of cool stuff."

**Loral Langemeier:**

So, two tickets to the virtual meetup and marketplace. You're also going to get two tickets Off Wall Street. That's when we go back out live, once we get back to whatever normal is. We are saying now sometime in July, we believe people will fly in to either Reno or Vegas, which are our two Nevada towns, because that's where I'm staying. I'm taking the opportunity to come home. And I have a 13 year old and a 20 year old and he's a big NCAA college football player and I'm going to go watch my son play ball off ball. It's going to be super fun. I'm going down to Georgia.

**Loral Langemeier:**

So you're going to get tickets, you're going to come out and see us. You're going to have critical to prepare, we have what's called fast cash coaching. So it's three live calls a week, it's Monday, Wednesday, and Thursday and it's live with high, high, high skilled marketing sales trainers. So it's not pre recorded. You come live and you say, "Okay, I got to work on my phone, I got to work on my offer." And you practice making money to get ready for the marketplace.

**Loral Langemeier:**

When you come to our Offline Wall Street, we do a marketplace there. And I guarantee you I'll make money at that one for sure. We actually put together a four hour course. So with the detail of our conversation today, but really, really in detail with some scripts. We are going to give you a whole process for how to create a business model, how to update your sales funnel, learn that sales versus serving. You see you're going to actually learn that and here's what I can tell you about, and I got to address this, especially because I just, I love Raymond's audience. I love coming out and speaking to him, but I can tell you this, too many of you are lying to yourselves saying, "Oh, I have a weird mindset with money." No, you don't. You don't know how to sell.

**Loral Langemeier:**

You can have the greatest like, it isn't about your mindset, whether you have a checkbook or not. It's whether you've asked for the money, right? What do you need? How can I help you? And then I say, I call it ask, so I'm going to say, "Francis, how can I help you with money?" You're going to tell me what you need Francis. I'm going to tell you why, I'm going to help solve it. And I'm going to say, do you want to wire? Give me credit card or cryptocurrency? How do you want to pay me? And the reason you don't have money isn't because you have a screwed up relationship to money, it's because you don't have to ask for it and you don't have an offer that serves other people's lives.

**Loral Langemeier:**

So there's the harsh truth and it's the real truth. And what happens when you start making money, your mindset, everything has to change because it has to catch up to it. You're going to be a part of our marketplace and we're going to continue to do marketplaces.

**Loral Langemeier:**

I created this cool thing during our marketplace where we stayed together and Dominic and Rachel were part of it. It's called Zaphter hours because a thing I miss the most when I went out to shows is I missed the after hours. I miss being with people. I am so connected to people. Like when you're my client, you get my cell phone. Like I want to know what's going on, I want to stay engaged. It's probably what's created all my experience. So I miss the after hours. So I got, bought the URLs Zaphter hours. So it's Zaphter hours on Zoom. And every once in a while, we're just like last night we did a Zaphter hours. Like, "Hey, who wants to go Zaphter hours."

**Loral Langemeier:**

And I don't know, 40, 50 people come up, and we just talk, we just talked about money. So that'll be part of that unique marketplace is just staying in connection and having these money conversations. I'm going to show you how to get funding. And I can tell you in Canada, well, most of the time, some of the banks in Canada, if you know where to go are giving anywhere between 20,000 to $1.7 million to help your business stay alive or fund them.

**Loral Langemeier:**

Again, you've got to start your money rolls. So some of you are being entrepreneurs, that's your new thing. Like you got to think yourself and you're in again, one of three spots. You're totally barely getting it together. You're laid off and you're becoming an entrepreneur, and then you have money. So having money means you need some money rules and ideas, where are you going to put it? And you can prioritize. So don't follow my rules. Let's help you get your rules so you have the confidence in a big conversation and standing with it, and then how to participate.

**Loral Langemeier:**

And the way we're going to do that is through a lot of conversations. We're going to continue to invite you as a client, we will be doing conversations, not only the fast cash ones, but those after hours with me, and other of our top instructors and multimillionaires. Like there is a vehicle dealership, it's outside of Dallas, Texas, and we're going to very, very clearly dissect to you how we're going to go buy it.

**Loral Langemeier:**

And so I'm very transparent about the stuff that I'm looking at, or if I don't want it and you want to send it to me, let's dissect it together as a group, that's the best learning I've ever known to just live out and let's talk about money. And then you're going to engage where you need to engage.

**Loral Langemeier:**

So here's what's super cool, is all of this together. First of all, I have never even done all this stuff. A bonus that I already promised you, but I forgot to put it on the slide and I just, I have to, is I need you to come see us at a real estate tour. So that is like that a by itself is another $2,000 bonus. So when you sign up and here's the simple price today is 997 you're going to click on the link. So there's the link, you're going to click on the link and I believe, Francis you've got to correct me, I believe this was being run in . . . Is this US or Canadian? Because I know you guys are going to be running our orders.

**Francis:**

I will find out for you right now.

**Raymond Aaron:**

Everything is in Canadian, Loral.

**Loral Langemeier:**

That's what I thought, I thought it was in Canadian. So this is a ripping deal, ripping deal. I wouldn't have done that. But I knew, it's fine. It's not even about that. I want to change your life. I want you in my marketplace. I'm going to show you. I want you your eyes wide open going, "Oh my gosh."

**Loral Langemeier:**

See my passion with all of this and I'm going to get it done, this was my pivot to this as well. This needs to be homeschool courses. This needs to be in the school system. We need to be teaching the kids, I'm teaching you as adults, in junior high, six, seventh and eighth graders need to have this information armed before they go out into the world and it needs to happen before they get into high schools.

**Loral Langemeier:**

So that's where my passion is, at this point in my life. I love teaching it, I know how to do it. And so it's 997 Canadian, I don't know Raymond if you guys want to take payment plans. However, you want to do it, I am completely open, I would just like to serve your group and see them at a marketplace, see them virtually, and then see them live when we come live, and see them in a real estate tour. And if takes a year to use all this stuff, we'll take a year.

**Loral Langemeier:**

So it's not about the time, it's about your commitment and doing it now, because you have no reason, you have no distractions, but to learn money. So Raymond, thank you for letting me be on and if there's questions, Francis, I'll see it right here and answer further questions.

**Raymond Aaron:**

Loral, you are like a whirlwind. You're like a human hurricane. That I just never experienced anything so dazzling. Aaron. com/financialkit please spell my name correctly, aaron.com/financialkit. Loral will take you by the hand, give you dozens of green tick marks that she shows you there, plus she's going to take you on a real estate tour that she didn't even mention. It's normally 2,000 US dollars, she reduced it to 997 US before she realized we were offering it in Canadian dollars so you got another 35% discount. This is insane to get Loral Langemeier the star the movie The Secret, the millionaire maker herself and all those items for 997 Canadian it's crazy simple just do it. Just do it. So Francis-

**Loral Langemeier:**

Here's what I can guarantee, they won't see that offer again. They might see a little part of it back at retail but yeah because that's really for us, right? It's more like, what, 700 bucks US?

**Raymond Aaron:**

Yeah.

**Loral Langemeier:**

It's crazy. You can't even go on a real estate tour for that, you can't do any of this for that. So join in. I do want to do one variance for some of you because I have been to Toronto a lot, and obviously back and forth in Calgary a lot. If you happen have an off Wall Street ticket, don't make it all complicated for Aaron and his team. Just you know what, take the two extra tickets and give them to somebody or sell them to somebody and make money.

**Loral Langemeier:**

I mean, just the off Wall Street tickets alone are worth 750 each, that's 1500 if you would buy them on a live stage. So don't say, "Oh, I already have tickets." Good, take two more, go sell them to somebody or give them away as a COVID gift and don't, I just wanted to say that Raymond because I was looking at like what we'd get offered before and none of this has been offered but that and I don't want you to get all weird if some of your viewers are like, "I already have it." Well good, go sell them or give them away, but take the whole thing.

**Raymond Aaron:**

Amazing. You're amazing. Aaron.com spell my name correctly or it won't work, aaron.com/financialkit to get dozens of her amazing items and the extra one that she added, the real estate tour not for 3000 US, not for 1000 US which is what she thought, but for 997 Canadian, that's it's crazy low. Crazy, crazy low. It's a special COVID deal, grab it.

**Loral Langemeier:**

It's a Raymond Aaron deal because I love you.

**Raymond Aaron:**

Well, you're special in my heart. Francis, do we have some questions or should I go on? By the way, if you're still here, wait for a few minutes because I want to . . . After we finish with Loral

I wanted to summarize the entire event. So just stay for another five or 10 minutes, we'll finish with Loral, answer questions and then I'll just summarize it.

**Francis:**

Lots of questions. And remember, there is a delay on the social media streams. So we'll get questions from there in a second. But on our live chat here, let's see. I don't have a business yet I'm learning to start a business, can you help me?

**Loral Langemeier:**

That's what the marketplace is, from start to finish, you will . . . here's how fast your 48 hours is going to go May 13th, 14th, 15th. First of all, you're going to sign up today, and it's Friday. So by Monday at five o'clock, as long as we transfer all of our clients, by Monday at five o'clock Pacific, you will be on your first phone call that fast cash call, and we are going to help you pick a business if you don't have one. If you need business ideas, we got plenty of them. And you will pick a business. You are going to learn a funnel, you're going to learn to price, and you will learn to sell and by the marketplace you will be making money, and I will force you to make money.

**Loral Langemeier:**

So it doesn't matter that you don't know and if your kids don't know. What's fun about the kids, is they have their own conversations but what was really interesting about this time because we're so family oriented. I mean, even when I'm married now my kids, I still have 13 to 20 year old and we commute a lot. So, essentially I raised Mike is a single mom. My point is, they have played, they have been involved, they are involved. My son even said, "You know, I need to go teach these kids because they're so not there."

**Loral Langemeier:**

But what was awesome is to watch a 16 year old sell a 60 year old an item, right? It was awesome to watch a six year old sell a 20 year old an item. So it's a pretty indiscriminate marketplace right now. I think it's leveling the playing field, and everybody realizing they can really do anything they want right now.

**Francis:**

Outstanding, I guess as a follow up question here from Juanita, is this in reference to any kind of business?

**Loral Langemeier:**

Yes, yep. That's, because I have been a millionaire in many, many ways. I mean, real estate, gas and oil businesses. I have flipped a business. I love flipping businesses. I love picking up little broken businesses and growing them up. In fact, the Canadian company that's still pays me dividends is called Vetrazzo. We picked it up out of Berkeley, California. It's a broken little glass company, a client of mine found it. I thought, that's awesome. It's a green product. It's awesome. We went through 2008, '9, we had a huge financial catastrophe in the middle. We sold it to a Canadian company, we kept what I call a trail. So yes, it applies to anything.

**Loral Langemeier:**

I have owned so many different things, and have so much different experience. And if I don't know how to do it, believe me, I can find one person and one phone call to go tell you how to do it. So there's not a business that I'm scared of, there's nothing . . . And so if you want to consultant we're not that. We're not going to come run your company for you. We're not like that. We are going to strategize your company for you and with you, but we're going to teach you to fish so you don't need us.

**Loral Langemeier:**

I think it's really disabling when people do too much for you, not as a team but as the strategist. My goal is to have you be amazing entrepreneur and investor.

**Raymond Aaron:**

And just in case you weren't understanding what she said when she said a broken glass company. It was a glass manufacturing company that was in trouble. It wasn't a company that sells broken glass, just wanted to be clear.

**Loral Langemeier:**

Yeah, and actually yeah, it was all free. Like we would go around, we'd pick up broken traffic lights, we would pick up beer bottles and sky blue vodka bottles and we would put this beautiful broken glass together in this resin. And it would make granite countertops and I have one. I have a beautiful one made out of red, yellow and green stoplights. And it's just this beautiful material. It can make tiles, it's just this beautiful . . . Yeah, I guess you're right, I was just using my internal knowledge saying broken glass company. But yes, broken glass and we made millions out of it.

**Raymond Aaron:**

Wow. Francis?

**Francis:**

Here's a surprise question. Did Loral say $997 Canadian dollars?

**Raymond Aaron:**

Yeah.

**Francis:**

It is correct.

**Loral Langemeier:**

$997 Canadian

**Raymond Aaron:**

Intentionally, she thought she was saying 997 US and then we have everything Canadian. So you get an inadvertent 35% discount or roughly that.

**Francis:**

Wonderful. Raymond I'll pass it back to you.

**Raymond Aaron:**

Okay, Loral thank you so much, you were amazing. I'm glad you finished off our day. I'm just going to spend five minutes recapping it for everybody. Thank you for coming. Big, big giant hug to you.

**Loral Langemeier:**

Thank you, love you. Look forward to working with all of you. Take this step, this is critical that you and your family learn this at this time.

**Raymond Aaron:**

Yes, and by the way, many, many of my clients have . . . I've encouraged them to join Loral's programs because she is the millionaire maker. She will grab you by your hair and drag you to wealth. She will push you into owning a company like she is ruthless and you no matter what objections you have, she will make you a success. It's dazzling.

**Raymond Aaron:**

And to get all that for a few hundred Canadian, it's dazzling, it's just dazzling. So let me just say a few things, number one-

**Loral Langemeier:**

Can I add one and I promise I'll leave and be quiet. Raymond and I have this very sweet deal. And some of the folks that I've met along my journey is that when you do your books with him, because he does, I just have to say, there's so many people who will promise you a book, and I've seen that catastrophe. His team does an amazing job. And if you want, and I know that I've still offered to forward or endorse your book, if you're also a co-client, so that's an extra little bonus that I just wanted to put out there. I mean, I just ran into somebody recently. He's like, "Oh, my gosh." And that I had never really physically met him before, but because of our relationship, so I just want to honor you in that because thank God, you help people get a book really out instead of the promise and five years later they don't have a book. But I will still love to do that with any of the clients if they would like my forward on their book that is published with you only.

**Raymond Aaron:**

So that's another bonus when you get her program therefore, you're a client of hers and mine, you can have either me right your forward or Loral, at New York Times number one bestselling author and the star of The Secret. Wow, her or me, wow, wow, wow. Oh my God, thank you for adding that Loral.

www.ingramcontent.com/pod-product-compliance
Lightning Source LLC
Chambersburg PA
CBHW060045100426
42742CB00014B/2704